THE INCONVENIENT TRUTH ABOUT Business Success

Global Publishing Group
Australia • New Zealand • Singapore • America • London

THE INCONVENIENT TRUTH ABOUT Business Success

The 7 Reasons Why Most Business Owners Do Not Become Millionaires and The 1 Simple Thing That Can Change That

IAN MARSH

DISCLAIMER

All the information, techniques, skills and concepts contained within this publication are of the nature of general comment only and are not in any way recommended as individual advice. The intent is to offer a variety of information to provide a wider range of choices now and in the future, recognising that we all have widely diverse circumstances and viewpoints. Should any reader choose to make use of the information contained herein, this is their decision, and the contributors (and their companies), authors and publishers do not assume any responsibilities whatsoever under any condition or circumstances. It is recommended that the reader obtain their own independent advice.

First Edition 2015

National Library of Australia
Cataloguing-in-Publication entry:

Creator: Marsh, Ian, author.

The Inconvenient Truth About Business Success: The 7 Reasons Why Most Business Owners Do Not Become Multi-Millionaires And The 1 Simple Thing That Can Change That / Ian Marsh.

1st ed.

ISBN: 9781925288100 (paperback)

Small business – Australia – Management.
Business planning – Australia.
Success in business –Australia

Dewey Number: 658.0220994

Published by Global Publishing Group
PO Box 517 Mt Evelyn, Victoria 3796 Australia
Email info@GlobalPublishingGroup.com.au

For further information about orders:
Phone: +61 3 9739 4686 or Fax +61 3 8648 6871

I would like to dedicate this book to my wife Jenny, without whose love and support I would have never been able to achieve the successes that I have had.

I would like to tell my son Ian and daughter Brooke how much they mean to me and to acknowledge my mother Patricia and my father Ian, who gave me the internal principles that I live by today.

IAN MARSH

Acknowledgements

It has been an honour and privilege to write this book and as with any major project, there are a number of very special people who contributed to making this book happen. So, I'd like to take this opportunity to say "THANK YOU."

Firstly, I'd like to thank my first mentor, Mal Emery, who opened my eyes to the world of business.

A special thank you to the clients that I have helped over the years because your success is my success and the motivation you give me with the progress you make causes me to jump out of bed every day to see who else I can help! It has been an honour and a tremendous privilege to work with every one of you and I'm sure that thousands of people's lives will be influenced by the stories and insights that you've shared.

A special thank you to my mum and dad, Patricia and Ian, for the life lessons you taught me.

To my son and daughter, Ian and Brooke, whom I love with all my heart and soul.

A huge thank you to my publisher, Global Publishing Group and their awesome team for their dedication and commitment to the book's success.

And finally, I thank my beautiful wife Jenny who is my ultimate source of love, hope, courage and understanding on my continuous journey to success. I'm truly grateful for your absolute faith and trust in everything that I do and for keeping up with me during the challenging moments. You're simply one-of-a-kind and I love you for that.

FREE BONUS GIFT

Valued at $2,158 – But Yours FREE!

Claim your **FREE BONUS GIFT** by going to
www.workonthebusiness.com

I know you're interested in taking your business to the next level or you wouldn't be reading this book right now.

To help start you on the 'right track' I'd like to gift you a **FREE 2 month membership to our StreetSmart Business Success Club** (Valued at $2,158) All I ask is that you pay $9.95 towards P&H to cover the cost of posting this direct to your home or business.

You will receive:	**Valued at**
StreetPress Magazine & Success Module Workbook Filled with practical and PROVEN ideas and strategies that will help you grow your business. Inside StreetPress you will find your 'Success Club' module workbook helping you nail a key transformational business process.	**$54**
Success Training Module DVD To accompany your workbook, this training DVD steps out the module strategies in real time with real life examples for maximum benefit.	**$197**
Accountability Call This will ensure you actually implement the knowledge you receive.	**$50**
Hour of Power 'Ask Ian' Q & A With Ian Marsh Join a live webinar to ask Ian any pressing questions about your business and the current training module.	**$560**
EXTRA BONUS #1: One Day Business Mastery Live Training where you will learn ideas and strategies that could potentially add $1000's to your bottom line. (Clients pay $997 p/mth to be part of this powerful environment).	**$997**
EXTRA BONUS #2: A Business Acceleration Call where, if you have a viable operating business, one of my 'Business Growth Consultants' will uncover at least $30,000 of hidden profits.	**$300**
TOTAL VALUE (But yours for only $9.95 P&H)	**$2,158**

Claim your **FREE BONUS GIFT** today and create your own multi-million dollar business starting today by visiting **www.workonthebusiness.com**

Contents

Introduction

If you're reading the first page of this book, chances are that you're looking for answers to some challenge in your business.

You're probably a business owner and you're looking for a solution to a problem. I don't know what that problem is however, the purpose of me putting my experiences and my knowledge into these pages is to help serious individuals like you, who have a suspicion that they can achieve more and reach their potential if only they had some answers to the missing links that they've been searching for but haven't found. If that is the case, then you are reading the right book.

I want to state for the record that I'm not one of those wannabe individuals who have not really accomplished much in their business life and decided to get a book out there so that they can gain notoriety. There is not much that I have not experienced in business and I sincerely want this book to mean something and to have an impact on business owners out there because I personally know the risks, the challenges and the price that you have to pay every day. You have had the courage to put everything on the line and start working for yourself to create your dream, and for that I salute you.

I am going to share with you the inconvenient truth about being in business and why most individuals don't become multi-millionaires. Notice that I didn't say millionaires because quite frankly, a million dollars isn't that much anymore. I will share with you the philosophies that have helped me build five multi-million dollar companies and generate more money than I ever dreamed possible in my life. I do hope that my thoughts and philosophies help you on your journey to accomplish whatever it is you want in life.

I can assure you that if you have the courage to get serious about your business, it will reward you like no other opportunity on the planet. Please enjoy the following journey with me and when you are ready, I would love your feedback regarding the impact that this information has had on your life.

CHAPTER 1

So, Who Wants To Be A Multi-Millionaire?

CHAPTER 1

So, Who Wants To Be A Multi-Millionaire?

My story started many years ago when I was a youngster. You see, I always felt that I should be wealthy. I didn't come from wealthy parents. My parents always tried their best and really gave everything they could to their children. I didn't have a silver spoon in my mouth and my guess is that most people reading this book haven't either. To be quite honest, I had a strange upbringing. My parents were married seven times between them, which led to me having a very disruptive childhood and I experienced a lot of things that most children probably don't experience in life. This resulted in me deciding to leave home at the tender age of fourteen because I felt I could do a better job looking after my own destiny than my parents could. (There is a small chance I could have been wrong).

It's amazing how much you think you know at the age of fourteen and then realise how much you didn't know when you get to the age of twenty-five. Mum and Dad, I do apologise. I left home at the age of fourteen and went and signed on for an apprenticeship on the railways and decided that I'd become an electrician. Now, during those four years I was working towards my trade papers but quite honestly, I would never call myself a master tradesman.

By the end of four years I had been trained in what was probably one of the best possible environments to become a master tradesman, which was the State Rail Authority at the time. They had one of the most comprehensive training centres in Chullora which supported you with additional skills on top of TAFE, (paid by you, the tax payer, of course). You've got the teachers, you've got a dedicated training centre there to learn your skills and you have a trainer who is responsible for only thirty apprentices. Despite having all of these resources, by the time I left my apprenticeship the major skill that I had developed was how to drink a bottle of scotch in one night. That was my claim to fame (pretty sad). It's not something to be proud of, ladies and gentlemen, but let me tell you that this is a book on the inconvenient truth for both you and me and I cannot help you if I don't share and am not open with you about my past.

Let me say that by the time I finished my apprenticeship, the skills that I had mastered were definitely not those of the great tradesman. Now, why didn't I become a great tradesman, even though I had all of the resources and all of the opportunities in front of me? Well, quite simply, I just didn't have any desire to be a great tradesman. The reason I chose to be an electrician was simply because I thought girls might find that a bit cooler than if I was a plumber.

Anyway, moving on. After my apprenticeship, I decided I needed a bit of adventure in my life and went to join the army. I thought, "Hey, this'll be fun," so I joined the regular army but after a while I wanted a bit more adventure and I decided to apply to join the commandos. Please understand that I'm not built like Arnold Schwarzenegger, I'm just an average guy, but at the time the big action movies were coming out at the cinemas and Arnold Schwarzenegger was my hero, so I set my sights on becoming a commando. Sure enough, I got into the commandos despite what all my friends and family said to me, that being, "You've got no hope, buddy."

During my time in the 1st commando unit at Mosman, I learned how to do some pretty amazing things.

For those of you who don't know how the armed forces work, (now I'm talking infantry here), essentially, the powers-that-be decide that they want to defeat an enemy. To do this they need to destroy sensitive targets such as bridges, ammo dumps, communication centres etc.

Before they can destroy these things they need to know exactly where they are and how to eliminate them, so they send in the SAS. These guys really are super human and they go behind enemy lines, usually on their own, or perhaps one other member goes with them, to seek out where the best targets are, determine the coordinates and send them back to HQ and that is where we come in.

We generally go behind enemy lines in a squad of about six people and blow up the targets that the SAS have pinpointed. And That's what I learned to do, blow things up and get fitter and tougher than I ever thought possible. Really, become a lean, mean, killing machine full of testosterone.

It was quite an amazing time for me and I did enjoy it but did I become as good a soldier as I possibly could be? No. I did okay but there were a lot of people who were a lot better than I was. Why was that? Well, quite honestly, I never had the desire to become a lean, mean killing machine. I actually prefer to be a lover, not a fighter. So, it was time to leave and find another adventure.

I decided then, after the commandos, that maybe I would try to make some money. I thought, 'Hey, I've got my electrical license so why don't I get my contractor's license and get out there and do my best to make a dollar? Other people seem to make money as an electrical contractor, why can't I?'

So, off I went out there into the wide world of business with no clue to what I was doing and with the money that I had behind me, all I could afford was a beat-up Ford Escort Mini van, running on two cylinders with smoke pouring out of the back of it, as my first contracting vehicle.

I set off trying to find work and I actually got lucky when I joined a company called Spinners and subcontracted to them for quite a while. Remember the first part of this chapter when I told you that I was no amazing electrician? Well, I fumbled my way around trying to make a dollar but I wasn't very good at it. In fact, it was a real challenge for me just to stay alive and put food on the table.

Anyway, one day I was goofing off because I did not have any work to do and I was walking along the Darling Harbour Promenade when I saw these signs saying, "Money Expo." I said to myself, "Oh God! Money! I'd love to be exposed to some money. That'd be nice." This was the very first time I had ever seen an expo but when I excitedly tried to enter the exhibition, someone stopped me and had the gall to ask for $20.00 for the entry fee.

Well, I didn't have twenty dollars to my name but for some reason I knew that I had to get inside the exhibition to learn about money.

So, being a good, resourceful tradesman, I knew the tradesmen's entrances to most premises and I snuck in through the back of the exhibition centre trying to look like I belonged there. The fact that I was successful must have been due to my commando training. As I got in there, I saw a bald headed individual talking on a stage and I quietly tried to sit in the back and look inconspicuous. I have to admit that I looked like a bit of a mess because I couldn't afford decent clothing. I am talking dirty shirt, ripped jeans and sandshoes with hardly any soles. Anyway, I was listening to this individual starting to talk about being successful in business and a phrase came out of his mouth that I will never forget.

He said, "I've got no problem with someone being broke but I've got a real problem with them staying broke."

It was like a lightbulb went off in my head and I thought, "You know what? This guy's got the answer." I wrote down just about every word that came out of his mouth and after the presentation this individual made a beeline towards me and asked me for my name. I honestly thought that I'd been busted for coming in without paying and he was going to hit me up for the twenty dollars.

Actually, he just took my details and about a week later a book ended up at my front door. It was called, 'How to Turn an Ordinary Business into an Extraordinary One.' Now, that book and that mentor went on to change my life. I didn't know it at the time but that was a massive turning point in the future of Ian Marsh. You see, that individual up on stage was Mal Emery and he was the first mentor that I ever had in business. When he started talking, the things that he was saying really resonated with me and I felt like I had found my calling.

Okay, I'd admitted I didn't want to be an electrician, I wasn't that great and I'd admitted I didn't want to be a lean, mean, fighting machine, so I left that area. Now, listening to what I could do with marketing and sales and business, I knew that I'd found my calling. I'd found my mission and I knew that I wanted to be as good as I could be in mastering business. That was it. I was on a mission and I devoured the book that Mal sent me (probably out of pity). Remember, I didn't have any money at the time but the book had a story in it about FAI security and how this FAI company built themselves up from nothing to be the fastest growing security company in Australia simply because they did the right thing. Their tradesmen put booties onto their shoes before they walked in the door. They put drop sheets on the carpets from the front to the back of the house. If there were globes blown and if they had time, they would just change the globes for the client at no extra charge.

Looking at this example I thought, "Wow! That was an experience. Well, I can do that. I might not have money but I do have time." I started to apply the strategies in that book towards my clients. In fact, I went down to a place called Carpet Court in North Parramatta and I pleaded with them. I said, "Look, I haven't got any money but I really do need a bit of a hand. I'm hoping you have some scrap carpet that you're not going to use and which I could take off you. I want to use it for drop sheets when I see people in their homes."

The universe must have figured it was time to give me a break because it just so happened that the salesperson at the carpet centre said, "This crazy lady in Castle Hill got us to outfit her whole home with this beautiful red carpet. Then, when we'd done the whole job, she decided she didn't like the colour and we ripped it all up and the carpet is sitting in the back dump at the moment. You can help yourself to whatever you want." That was it! I got all this red carpet and I cut it into strips and rolled it all up and quite honestly, set forth to replicate the things that FAI did with their clients. I didn't have many resources but I had time and I wanted to make the most of it. So, when I went into people's homes, I got the rolls of red carpet out and I put my booties on and I rolled the carpet down the hallways. It was really like walking down the red carpet at the Academy Awards. You can imagine what the clients were thinking when they saw this.

On top of that, when I had time I would get little power point protection plugs and if I saw that someone had little babies or children, I would put the protection plugs into the power points and not charge them for it or I'd change their globes or, particularly with the pensioners, I would clean out their gutters even though they didn't ask me to. I knew they didn't have a lot of money and I wanted to help them out; it was the right thing to do. I didn't have a lot of clients at the time so I spent the time helping them out and I liked having cups of tea and scones.

Now you can imagine what the pensioner was thinking as I was helping with all of these wonderful tasks that they could no longer do. While I was out doing their gutters they were on the phone to their friends. There would be Mildred, Betty and Sue on the telephone to all their friends saying, "Listen, if you need an electrician, you've got to ring this guy. He's such a lovely person! Don't use anyone else. You wouldn't believe what he is doing for me right now and I didn't even ask him to." The next thing I knew, I got busier than ever trying to keep up with all of these pensioners asking me to fix things in their homes. I didn't charge them a lot of money and it was okay because going from pretty much zero to making what I was, was a big improvement.

My days filled up and soon it was chock-a-block full with helping these people, which was fantastic except for one thing. Pensioners don't have a lot of money so I was maxed out working for them but I was not making a big income. I did get an awful lot of cups of tea and scones and made a lot of friends though and it was how I started to make an income and started to get ahead.

To give you an idea of the impact this was having on my finances, I went from making around $300.00 a week to making $1,500 a week, and to me that was a fortune.

Now, you may think that with this money I would go and maybe try to buy a house or invest it in some savings place like all my friends and family told me to but I did not listen to them, I put it where I believe the best investment of all is. An investment that gives you thousands of percent return on your money. That was myself. You see, every bit of money that I made, I actually reinvested into educating myself. There were some challenges with me doing that and I'll talk about that in a little while but, needless to say, I started to improve my knowledge on what it takes to be successful in business.

Now, here's the inconvenient truth about business owners. Only 7% of business owners ever reach a million dollars in turnover. Only 5% of individuals ever earn more than $140,000 and the worst statistic of all is that ONLY 39% OF BUSINESSES MAKE A PROFIT! Why is that?

Well, I'm guessing that they probably had a similar start to me when they started in business. That is, they had no idea how to create a successful business and they were just winging it. Essentially, that was how I started to make a success and how I started to get some income coming into my company. In the next chapter I share how I learned to make SERIOUS money but before you read it, please read these inconvenient truths!

INCONVENIENT TRUTH

You do not know what you don't know!

You understand that other people are making 10 times more money than you are without working 10 times harder and that you have the ability and the right to do the same but you need the courage to believe it can happen.

You are living in a reality that you created!

For you to break through to another reality you need to commit to opening up to different thought processes and the possibility of different outcomes than the ones you are used to.

CHAPTER 2

Creating The Vision

CHAPTER 2

Creating The Vision

My life started to turn around when I started to invest in myself and started to learn the things that other people knew and that I didn't. I started to get results that I didn't think were possible. I never actually thought that I'd be able to fill up my appointment book with work. That was the start of a new life for me. Even though I wasn't making a lot of money, I was making decent money and I was really starting to gain a bit more confidence in myself.

It is quite amazing how the world works in that, when you do something and it works, it motivates you to do more of it and so become better at it.

The problem is that the exact opposite is also true. When you try something and it doesn't work you do less of it and believe you are no good at that thing or that the strategy doesn't work.

Here is an example of what I mean. Let's say you decide to create a direct mail marketing strategy and you use postcards to get your message out there.

You decide to do your own copywriting instead of hiring a professional copywriter and learning the principles of direct mail, you decide you know better and you mail 1,000 postcards then sit by the phone waiting for it to ring. After a few days, when you get no response, your mind says to you, "You see, I told you, direct mail doesn't work, you just wasted $1,500 you idiot. Do not do that again!"

Now, let's look at the same scenario but through the eyes of a streetsmart business owner who has learned these core principles of direct mail.

Get professional copywriters to write your copy, only expect a 0.5% response rate and always be prepared to send at least 3 mail-outs to the same people or do not even start the campaign. You must realise that it is far better to mail 5,000 people three times than to mail 15,000 people once.

This business owner waits by the phone and gets the 25 leads that he was expecting (0.5% response rate).

What the streetsmart business owner's mind tells him is, "I told you that you were a genius! Look at all these leads, now all we need to do is increase the size of the mail-out and we will get double the result. Well done! How soon can we do this again?"

This cycle is what traps people into their belief systems and you need to be aware of this so that you do not become a victim of it.

Below is a diagram of this in action. I learned this from Tony Robbins many years ago and know just how true it is.

Looking at the diagram below, imagine the two business owners doing their direct mail postcards. Both had the potential to make it a success. They both took action. One took the right action and followed professional advice and the other made a half-hearted attempt.

Then they both got a result, one had a great result and the other had a bad result.

Then they both created belief systems. One decided that postcards are fantastic and the other believed that they don't work.

As crazy as this sounds, they are both right. Here is the secret. You get to decide what you want your outcome to be, by your actions.

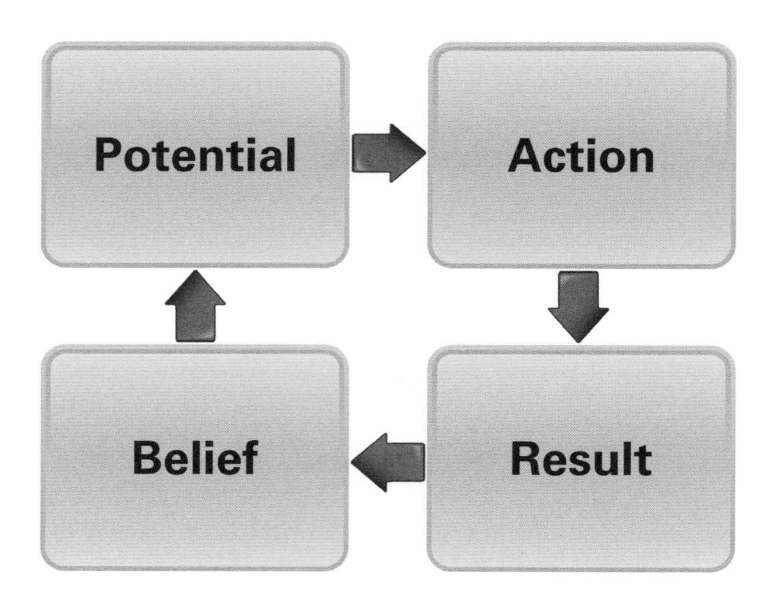

Just like it happens in life, when you get serious about things and you know what you want and you start feeling good about the effort that you're putting into your life, better things seem to happen. Good things attract more good things, just like bad things attract more bad things.

Anyway, back to my story about how I started getting my act together. I met a beautiful woman! Yes, it happens with most guys but remember that I had parents who had been married 7 times and so I was being very careful about the woman I chose to be my wife. She had to be the right person and someone I wanted to spend the rest of my life with. Finally, at the age of 33, I found her. Her name is Jenny and when I asked her out she actually said yes. This was quite an amazing experience for me because deep down, I knew that I had found the woman that I wanted to spend the rest of my life with.

As time went on, I knew without a doubt that this was the woman that I wanted to marry but being realistic about my attributes and current financial state, I thought that me getting down on one knee and saying "Please marry me" to Jenny, didn't really have a high probability of success. However, I knew that I wanted to provide a better life for Jenny so I decided to get serious about what I wanted to create in life, not so much for me but for this woman of my dreams. I also wanted to dramatically increase my chances of her saying yes to my marriage proposal.

One Friday afternoon I rang Jenny and said "Honey, I want to take you away for an amazing weekend." Jenny replied, "Oh fantastic. I'll get ready. What should I wear?" I said "Oh, just get dressed mid-range. Don't get dressed up too classy but don't wear thongs and jeans. Just dress nicely because we're going to be meeting some very interesting people this weekend." Well, you can imagine Jenny's curiosity. She thought that we were going to have a wonderful weekend away and go to a party with interesting people.

When I turned up to fetch her, she was all excited and set for an incredible weekend away with her man. I'd built her expectations up pretty high, I must admit. When I saw her waiting there with those beautiful sparkling eyes and almost jumping out of her skin with excitement, I started to get worried about my great plan, but the die was cast.

So, then the questions came. "Okay, I am so excited, where are we off to? The central coast for the weekend? Or is it the Blue Mountains? I have my bag packed so c'mon, tell me what we are up to?" Well, now I was getting really worried but I put my best face on which wasn't easy to do and put as much excitement into my voice as possible and said, "Honey, this weekend I am going to take you on an amazing journey to our future life." I still remember the blank stare and the look of confusion. She was still smiling but then she said, "What are you talking about?" I replied, "Well, I'm going to show you the life that we're going to have together a few years down the track." She said, "You mean I got all dressed up, packed my bags and cancelled tomorrow's lunch with my friends so that you could take me on some make believe drive? You are joking, aren't you?" I told her I wasn't and I swear, I can still visualise the look of anger that came across her face. (Wow! That is a scary look!)

Anyway, as we were driving along, I said, "Honey, this will be a fantastic weekend. I know you're not that happy right now but please play a game with me. It is important. Just imagine that it's 2 years down the track and we are still together, what sort of home would you want us to live in?"

Again she said, "You are joking aren't you? You can't even afford to take me away for the weekend and you're asking about the type of house I want to live in?"

Jenny looked at me with this weird expression on her face and I have to admit that I was seriously starting to worry that I had blown my chances with my dream girl but I persevered with my plan. I said "Honey, come on, just humour me. What sort of house would you like to live in and what sort of things would you like to be doing?"

After a little time Jenny warmed up to this and said "Okay. I've always loved horses and had horses when I lived in Tamworth, so I'd really love to have a property with horses." I said "Oh, okay. How big would that property have to be?" Jenny said "It would have to be at least 5 acres." I said "Okay. Well, imagine that I could get you this property and it was on 5 acres. What else would it have to have on it? What would the house look like?" Jenny said, "Well ..." (she was starting to get into it now) she said, "I want to have 4 bedrooms and I want to have a swimming pool and while we're at it, I want a tennis court and I want to have facilities for my horses so that I can have 2 horses on the property." I said "Okay, if that's what you want, let's go and have a look at a few houses and see if we can find the house we want."

My girlfriend still had this really stunned look on her face and I am sure she was thinking, "Am I going out with a crazy person?" But, I pulled over, we had a cappuccino and looked in the paper for open houses. We circled the ones with potential and I started taking her to the open homes and properties, largely around Castle Hill and Dural and a place called Oakville, where these types of properties were common. So we started going to all the open homes we could find and Jenny was really starting to enjoy seeing these beautiful places.

At the end of the day, it looked like we would need to spend around $1.1 million to get the property that Jenny would love to live in.

Then I said to her, "This is the dream life that we want for our future, so we should have a look at dream cars. What sort of car would you like to be driving?" And it turned out that she was a big truck type of girl, Landcruisers, F250s etc. All these vehicles, as I later learned, were ideal for towing very expensive horse floats but this was my turn and so I didn't miss my chance. We spent the day test driving BMWs, Prados and other nice $100-$200k cars, getting pricing and deals from all the car dealers we could find. I eventually put down the Lexus convertible as my dream car and Jen wanted the Toyota top of the line Prado. So my car was around $180k and Jenny's car was $100k.

The next thing in our dream life was holidays so I said to Jen, "Alright, what sort of holidays would you like to have? If we went on holiday, how long would you like to go for and where would you like to go?" She said, "Well, I've always wanted to go to Europe and visit Paris and go on the canals and drink wine and cheese and go to the nice restaurants there."

So off we went again but this time we went to travel agents. We got all the information we needed about a trip to Paris and even found out how much it would cost. We really got serious with all of these things.

So that was how we spent the weekend and when we got back home we looked at how much that type of lifestyle would cost us.

You must understand that this was not exactly the perfect weekend that my girlfriend had envisioned at the time but in the end, Jenny had a great time. I am sure that she never believed for one minute that any of these things were possible but she humoured me and I got what I needed. By the end of the weekend I had a vision about the lifestyle I wanted to create for the most wonderful woman in the world. It became my passion, my mission if you like, to provide this for my future family.

So, I put all these things together in my goal book and started to create a plan to get them. Looking back, I have to admit that it's a wonder my girlfriend did not drop me or at least ask me to get professional help.

The story that I've just shared with you is a very personal one. I've shared it a few times but that journey that I took really set me on a trajectory to getting the things that I wanted in life. I'm going to tell you what happened with the things on that wish list fairly shortly but first let me ask if you have ever taken the time out or had the courage to really decide what you wanted in life. When was the last time that you got serious and said, "Well, is this the house I *want* to have or is this the house I *have* to have? Is this the holiday I *want* to have or is this the holiday I *have* to have? Is this the car I *want* to drive or is this the car I *have* to drive?"

It's your choice what car and what house you have and what life you want to lead but you need to decide what that is. If you don't know what you want in life, how are you ever going to get it? I urge you, as crazy as it may sound, to take a journey like I did. Work out what you really want in life. Get serious about it and work out exactly what sort of money you need to make in order to have these things.

With that being said, let me continue the journey. So, now that I had a vision of what Jenny wanted in life, I built up the expectation of what life would be like with me at her side but the next question was how I was going to be able to afford these things. After dropping Jenny off at her home and promising her that I would get these things for her one day, I sat at my dining room table and started doing the calculations to find out how much money I would need to create our dream life.

Now, after adding everything up, my reality set in and I had this horrible sick feeling deep in the pit of my stomach. When I worked it all out, I figured that I needed an income of $250,000 a year to create the dream life that we had just played out.

There are certain moments in life that are pivotal points and they have a massive impact on one's future. This was one of those moments. I felt the world implode around me and I started believing that I had just signed the death warrant on my relationship with Jenny. I mean, who was I kidding and how could I ever multiply my income by 5 times? That was for other people, not for me. It was time to crawl back under the rock I had poked my head out from.

But then another set of thoughts started to enter my mind. What about other people that have this type of life? There are millions of people that live like that and earn that kind of money and I have as much right to that kind of lifestyle as they do. I decided there and then that I was going to make that $250,000 so that I could provide for the love of my life and I would do whatever it took to make it happen.

Needless to say, I put my head down and my backside up and I started to work out a strategy to make our dreams a reality.

That was when I realised that the movie, The Matrix, is real (well sort of). You see, we're busy leading our lives right now and doing the things that we have to do in order to make the wheels go around. We've got to make sure that we pay the mortgage, that we've got food on the table, that we pay outrageous amounts to the tax man and do what's expected of us to have what we believe we should have in life. Now, there is an 80% chance that what you are doing right now is living the movie. The things that you are doing each and every day are really a movie that you have created for yourself. You've created your reality in many ways because you are exactly where you deserve to be in life, largely due to the choices and decisions that you have made.

In fact, those choices and decisions have brought you to this point where you are sitting in your chair, reading this book and turning these pages and listening to my thoughts because you are searching for something. I do not know what it is but you do. You know there is a piece missing in your life puzzle and you are on a search to find it. Yes, it is true. There is a red pill and a blue pill in life. If you want to stay in the life that you have, just swallow the blue pill and you'll continue doing what you've been doing up until now and you'll keep getting the results that you've been getting well into the future.

On the other hand, you could swallow the red pill. If you have the courage to swallow the red pill and start taking this inconvenient journey with me and creating the life that you want rather than the one you feel you have to have, miracles will start to occur. The brick walls that you think surround you and keep you in the life you have to have, will start collapsing.

You'll be able to break through those brick walls and reach a whole new reality because right now, you really are living the fantasy of your own making.

Your world may be a very pretty one and it might even be a fantastic one but it is a world that you have created through your actions, your decisions and your efforts. What I want to explain to you is how this fantasy world that you're living in right now has been created and how you can create a new fantasy world for yourself if you are serious about change.

The best way to do this is to tell you a story about a person who was raised by a really lovely couple. They were office workers. Their names were Mary and John and they lived on a salary of $70,000 each.

They had a son called Pete and they raised him like most middle class families do. John grew up seeing all these wonderful things that are out there in life and at the age of 20 when he finished school, he went to his parents, Mary and John, and said "Mum, Dad, I want to go into business and make a million dollars a year so that I can live the life of the people I see at the yacht club and be able to travel the world. Can you please help me get started?" Now Mary and John looked at their son in disbelief for a second and then started laughing hysterically as if Pete had just told a joke.

But then, after a few minutes, they realised Pete was not joking and that he expected them to help him get a start in a successful business.

Here's the point. For parents that never earned more than say 70, 80 or $100,000 a year in their life, they can't believe that their son has the ability to earn a million dollars a year. They've lived in their reality all their life and they've created their world with a belief system where $100,000 to $150,000 a year is a possible goal for their son and they want to protect him from foolishness.

Now, let me digress for a second and tell you a story that you all know and that is the story of Roger Bannister breaking the four minute mile. So, right throughout history we had doctors, physiologists and scientists telling the world that there was no way that anyone could run the mile in less than four minutes. For decades and decades this held true.

There were individuals out there who had tried to break the four minute mile and they had failed. Although, I'm guessing, back in prehistoric times if a caveman had a lion chasing him there's a good chance he would have broken the four minute mile before Roger Bannister did but I've got no proof of that fact so we'll just have to stay with the statistics that we know.

Now, although there was all the proof in the world that the four minute mile was impossible, Roger Bannister decided not to listen to all of the reasons why people couldn't run a four minute mile and he decided to work on reasons why he could run one. Sure enough, you all know that he did break the four minute mile and as soon as he broke it, it got broken by other individuals at least 12 more times that year, simply because they were now living in a new reality.

Did you know that John F Kennedy had no idea how to get to the moon when he made that famous speech, "We will go to the moon!" on May 25, 1961? He created a whole new reality when he put that idea out there and because of this we now have Richard Branson creating Virgin Galactic and within 5 years you will be able to get from London to Sydney in 1 hour (yup, it's true).

To really help you cement this concept into your mind, imagine that instead of Pete going to John and Mary and saying, "Hey, I want to make a million dollars a year in business," you had James Packer going to his now dead dad, Kerry Packer, and saying "Dad, I want to make a million dollars a year in business." Now, if you knew Kerry Packer and you're old enough to remember the style of individual he was, you could imagine what would come out of his mouth. It would be something like, "Shit son, is that as high as you've set your goals? Why did you only settle on a million dollars a year for yourself? Haven't I taught you better than that?" It would be the same with Rupert Murdoch and his son Lachlan or Donald Trump and his daughter Ivanka. In fact, Ivanka's a very independent young lady and she makes around 6 million dollars a year for herself after her lifestyle and costs; without dad's help because she's an accomplished model and business person in her own right.

So, for you to succeed you must accept that most of what is holding you back is the level of thinking that you currently operate at. You have a set of belief systems that are preventing you from achieving what is possible for you in your life. Before you can succeed and become a multi-millionaire you **need to believe that you are worthy of having and achieving whatever you want in life and have the courage to get out there and grab it**.

You've got to break through the barriers and start believing that you can have the things that you truly desire in life. Will they fall into your lap as the movie, 'The Secret,' tells you they will? NO, and nor should they! Life is fairly simple, you usually get out of it what you put into it. Now, I would just like to refer to 'The Secret' again for a second, if I may. This is a movie that was made by a lady who transformed her life by creating a story called 'The Secret,' which you can buy or watch on YouTube. It essentially says that if you sit under a palm tree and wish hard enough for things to come into your life, they will manifest themselves and you can attract anything that you want into your life and you will have it because you love it.

Unfortunately, that's only half the story. They left the part out about hard work. Let's face it, it's called work for a reason. The real equation of 'The Secret' is knowing what you want, believing that you can get it and then doing whatever it takes to achieve it.

So, how do you start the thought processes that get you into the right frame of mind so that you can start achieving the things that you want in life?

Your first step should be to find a mentor, someone that you can believe in, not just an individual who wants to separate you from your money (and no, this is not a sales pitch). Remember that I told you about my first mentor and how he put me on the right path? Well, every mentor has a mentor.

How do you find the right mentor? There are many individuals around who are happy to help you to grow when they know you are serious about what you want. But a word of caution, there are also many who will tell you that they can help you and they take your money but deliver very little.

My recommendation is that when you look for a mentor, look for someone who's at least five times more successful than you are in a particular field and look at their track record.

If I want to have a mentor in accounting and somebody to give me great advice, I won't go to a business mentor, I'll go to one of the best accountants that I can find. If I want to get the best legal advice, I want to find a mentor who's one of the most successful lawyers in town. I think you get where I'm coming from. Make sure that you see an individual who is truly successful in the area that you are searching for and then you'll be able to trust their advice.

This brings me to another point and that is regarding the influences in your life. When you've gone through life, and I'm sure you've had the same experience that I have, you've come up with a great idea but you make the stupid mistake of going and asking your friends, family and even your loved ones what they think of the idea. Even though you may think that's a good place to start for a sounding board, if they've never earned more than $80,000 or $100,000 in their life or if they've never owned a business or if they've never achieved massive success in their world or if they don't have a $10,000,000 property portfolio, why would you seek their guidance on something? If they're at the same level as you, how can you expect to get better advice and guidance from them than what you come up with yourself? Their quality of decisions got them to their station in life and it's pretty much at the same level as you are at.

How can they help you excel when they have not gained the knowledge to start excelling themselves? If truth be told, and you may not want to hear this but once again, the name of this book is The Inconvenient Truth, many people who are close to you secretly don't want you to succeed because if you succeed you're going to go to another level. That level may take you away from their circle of influence and where they're comfortable with you in their world and their group and quite honestly, they have a fear that if you become more successful than they are, they may lose you as a friend.

If they're in a world that circulates where they're used to making $80,000 or $100,000 a year and you build a successful business where you become a multi-millionaire, earning $500k or more, there is a chance that you're going to start hanging out in different social circles. They don't want that to happen. They want you to stay with them. They will never admit it but deep down they want you to stay in the sort of life that you have because most people are scared of change.

Let me give you a real life example of the risks of asking the wrong person for their opinion. It was the year 2007 and I had just started my first consulting business called Tradesman Profits. And, as with most people who start off in a new vocation, my first efforts were less than spectacular. In fact, I still remember my first public speaking gig. I managed to gather 12 plumbers into the back of a pub for the first seminar I had ever run and I was going to show them how much I could help them transform their business.

So, the stage was set, all 12 tradies are politely in their seats, I got on stage to share my words of wisdom and I opened my mouth but nothing came out. I had stage fright. I was looking at them and they were looking at me but no words were being exchanged!

I thought, "Oh boy, this is going great" when luck would have it that at that very moment, when I thought my career as a consultant was going to be very short lived, a very cute barmaid flashed me a smile through a serving hole in the back of the seminar room and these words came gushing out of my mouth, "Who wants a beer?" With that, I was downing schooners of VB with the other tradies and in between gulps, advising them on how they should be running their business.

I actually made $12,000.00 that night but I was very lucky. I knew that if I wanted to make it in this world I had to improve my communication skills. And sure enough, at the next training session that I did with my first mentor, Mal Emery, there was a gentleman there called Joel Bauer, who was an incredible master of public speaking and he offered a platform speaking course for $15,000.

Well, I thought, "Hallelujah! My prayers have been answered." I will do this training and improve my speaking skills.

I was all excited when I got home and shared the great news with my wife that I was lucky enough to learn from one of the greatest platform speakers on the planet and do his training and it only cost $15,000.

Well, I am afraid the news did not go down as well as I'd hoped. In fact, it earned me about a week in the sin bin, if you know what I mean guys. Being an entrepreneur can be very hazardous to your sex life but even though my wife was against it, I went to the training and at my next seminar I made $50,000.

I went, "YAHOOO! That was great!" So I figured that if I repeated the class, I may get an even better result. So I went to kind, paternal Mal and said, "You know how I just paid you $15,000 for the training? Well, it was great, I made $50,000.00 but I heard you were doing another course. Can I go again?" Mal said, "Of course, Ian." I then said, "Mal, is there any chance I can get a discount?" And Mal said "Of course not, Ian." Aah, C'est la vie.

You can imagine the conversation when I saw my wife and proudly told her I was doing the course again. (Yes guys, another week in the sin bin). But I have to say, I can't blame her for being upset. I tend to have this effect on people.

But, here is the kicker. At the next workshop I ran, I made over $300,000 in sales and these days I make $1,500,000 on weekends when I put on large events.

So, have you worked out the moral of the story yet? And yes, every word of it is true. At the time, my wife had no way of forming an educated opinion about my decision to invest $30k in my speaking skills but if I had listened to her (Remember, I love this woman more than life itself) I would not have been able to create the life for us that we enjoy now. One small choice and one moment when I decided that I was in control of my own destiny and knew what I had to do for our future, despite how I was going to pay for doing it, has now created millions of dollars for us.

The easy choice would have been to listen to my wife and put the money in the bank and get 3% interest on it. The right choice was for me to invest in myself and in the end, because of my speaking abilities these days, I have generated at least $10,000,000.00 just from speaking on my feet. What is that as a return? A bit better than 3%.

Think about when you have had to make tough decisions. Have you been swayed by unqualified people into making the wrong decision and regretting it for the rest of your life?

Understand that in the early days, when I started taking this journey, I invested nearly everything I possessed back into my self-education. Quite honestly, I could have become a monk because I did spend an awful lot of time sleeping on the couch in our home because the arguments I had with Jenny were very traumatic. But I believed with all my heart and soul in the necessity of improving myself and as a result, the returns have been spectacular.

Thank goodness, these days I have built trust with my wife and she knows the benefits that occur when you invest in yourself, and she has grown as well, but in those early days she was dead set against most of the self-education and a lot of the crazy ideas, as she would put it, that I had.

You too will have people like that in your life, people who could stop you from achieving your dreams because they will tell you that you can't do it.

I was told that I would never be able to get an apprenticeship because I didn't have the grades required. I was told that I would never be able to work for myself because I've never had any training and that I'd never be able to create a successful business because I do not have any qualifications and I was also told that I would never get into the commandos because I am not built like a tank.

If I had listened to any of those people, I would not be here writing this book today and doing my best to help you create a new reality for yourself because these people influence you. They're the ones that you've talked to and communicated with all your life but they are at a certain level of success in their world and they haven't graduated above it. I need you to understand that if you want advice on something you must go to an expert in that field, to someone who has been successful.

Please do not have these dream crushers tell you it can't be done because chances are that your one idea, your one thought or that one epiphany that you had could very well transform your world but a well-meaning person close to you could shatter that for you and you will go on leading the life you feel you have to live rather than the one you want to live.

I think you can tell how passionate I am about this point because I have seen this occur time and time again when I'm helping business owners. The one member of the family, it could be the husband or the wife, can see the opportunity and can understand where they can go if they have the right knowledge and the right guidance and yet the other partner doesn't see it or refuses to look at it and sadly derails that person's progress.

Remember, this is your life. You are responsible for your future. Your decisions and your actions have taken you to where you are in life and you are at a turning point right now and starting to learn new realities and you need to take control of your life if you want it to be different from the one you have now. Otherwise, you're going to be living somebody else's life. Now if you want to live your partner's life, that's fine, I'm not here as a marriage counsellor but don't go crying in your soup when you don't achieve the things that you know you're capable of achieving.

It's up to you to decide whether you can do something or whether you can't do something. You must take 100% responsibility for your actions, your decisions and your future and when you take that responsibility, you start making massive strides towards the goals that you want to achieve.

INCONVENIENT TRUTH

Have you worked out what you really want in life?

What is your motivation for getting these things?

Are you sitting under a palm tree wishing for good things to happen to you or are you out there making good things happen?

Are you willing to do whatever it takes to make them a reality?

Are you willing to take 100% responsibility for your life and your family's future?

CHAPTER 3

Making The Vision A Reality

CHAPTER 3

Making The Vision A Reality

Creating multi-million dollar success habits

Now, as I referred to earlier in this book, the reason there are individuals that are ten times wealthier than you are and seem to achieve ten times more than you do is not because they're ten times smarter or because they work ten times harder. They simply have multi-million dollar success habits that they apply religiously to their life. They are fanatical about following their success routine because they have found something that has worked and they have improved on it and they have stuck to it and they have implemented it over and over and over again. In this chapter I'm going to be sharing my success habits with you, the habits that have helped me build five multi-million dollar companies and helped other individuals generate tens upon tens of millions of dollars in their companies.

This chapter is probably the most important chapter in the whole book because you are the sum of your habits and it is so easy to create bad habits and those bad habits can take you on a spiralling journey to a life of not having what you want. It is a little difficult to start developing success habits but those habits will help you achieve anything that you want in life and it does get easier.

So, I'll ask you a simple question. Is it worth just putting in 5% more effort and raising your standards by 5% so that you can have the life and world that you want rather than the one that has been developed for you? Well, I can only answer for myself but I'd say, 'Hell yeah!' I'm just going to share my success habits, which really do only take an extra 5% of effort, with you. It's not hard but it does take discipline to make sure that they become part of your life. So, the first thing that I want you to do is get clarity and be serious about what you want in your life.

I have created a simple worksheet at the back of this book for you. This is the starting point for you to swallow the red pill in life and start getting the things that you really want, whether it is the house, the car, the holiday, the school or the retirement. Maybe you would even like to have enough money so that you can go and help disadvantaged children in a third world country.

Whatever your dream, whatever your vision, it's one thing to think about it and have good feelings about it, everybody does that, but it's another thing to make it a reality. That's what I'm talking about here because you can kid anyone you like in life but you should never kid yourself.

When you are ready, please go to the worksheets at the back of this book. I want you to fill out the answers to the questions and work out why you want to have lots of money and why you want a business to generate a high income for you. I don't want vague generalities. I want meaningful specifics because money itself is not a very good motivator.

Now, the reason could be because you've always wanted that nice seven series BMW or you've always wanted to have that beautiful home that's in your mind or you want to have at least $2 million put away for retirement so that you can have a decent life after your working days are over.

Whatever your reasons are, they can't just be for the money. The money's just a measuring stick. The stronger your whys and the stronger your reasons for having the money, the bigger your chances of success. This is really a why table. Why do I want to be a multi-millionaire? If it's because you want to have a beautiful home, I want you to be specific about the home. Don't just say, 'Well, I want to have a big house.' No, be specific. I want to have a four bedroom home on three acres with a tennis court and swimming pool and it's going to be two stories with a pool pavilion and have its' own river. That's the sort of clarity that I want you to have for your vision. I want you to go out and find that type of home and I want you to get serious about that type of home if that's what you want. The same with the car. So don't just say well, I want a nice car. No. Tell your brain exactly what type of car you're going to have and believe you're going to have it. Put the name of that car down. Take the car for a test drive. Put those photos everywhere that you can.

Do the same with the holidays, the schools and the retirement. I want you to fill the table in believing 100%

that you really want those things and that you're going to do whatever it takes to get these things. Then in the next column I want you to put down the price of those items, how much they cost and what their market value is. In the next column, write down the payments that are required for buying these things. Then down at the bottom you'll determine whether you need to get a loan for that amount of money and what the repayments would be and what sort of income would you have to generate. Now, I do want to make a side note here. I am not a financial planner and I am not giving financial advice. I'm not saying go out and buy every do-dad under the sun. What I am saying is that if you want something in life, get it because to the best of my knowledge, we only get one time around on this planet. Nobody's come back to tell me differently even though I do believe in God. So make it count. Tomorrow's too late. If you want it, start making a plan to get it.

So please fill this table out and in your heart of hearts, the only things you put onto this table are the things that you're really passionately wanting to achieve in life. Okay, now that you've completed this table what's occurred is that you have a figure below. That figure could be $300,000, it could be $500,000 or it could be $1,000,000 a year. It doesn't matter what the figure is. What matters is that you're serious about achieving that income and that you believe whole heartedly that you can earn it. Okay, so now that you've got that figure, that's your dream figure. For argument's sake you're going to say, 'I want to make, $300,000 a year profit in my company,' so that you can have the things that you want in life. If that's the case, you now have a target and you know the sort of income that you have to make to have the things that you want. Now we're simply turning it from hoping it will happen to making sure it happens. This first step of putting it down on paper and creating a simple plan has increased your chances of having those things by 1,000%. Stand by - this is where goal setting comes in.

Now that you know what you want, you have your goals. You've said to yourself, 'Yes, I am serious.' The next step is for you to set a timeline for when you want those items. Now, they must be realistic and they must be achievable timelines. If you know that you want a house and that the house is going to cost a million dollars and that the repayments on the house will be $5,000 a month and that for you to have a $5,000 a month repayment, you need to have an income of $25,000 a month, then you need to say to yourself, 'How will I generate $25,000 a month in my business?'

Now that you've worked out that goal and found that you've got to earn $25,000 a month, which is near enough to $5,800 a week, once again, you have a target. Now let's break that target down.

Let's say that we do want to make $300,000 profit in our business. This probably seems like a lot of money to someone who is used to earning $100,000 a year so what we need to do is break this down into achievable chunks that do not seem impossible for your brain to believe.

Things I will get

Goal	Value	Repayment
House	$1,000,000	$5,000 pm
Car	$100,000	$1,200 pm
Annual Holiday	$24,000	$2,000 pm
Retirement	$30,000 pa	$2,500 pm
Total		$10,700pm
Income Required		$300,000

Reverse Engineering Plan

We will reverse engineer what we have to do to make that $300,000. For this exercise let's assume that you're selling an air conditioning system. That air con system costs $10,000 to buy. Now when you sell this system to someone you're going to make $3,000 profit on that system. Yes, for the sake of this exercise I'm not taking into account tax and all the other variables that may occur in life. I want to show you a simple, proven method for getting what you want out of life.

Here is a simple diagram to help your visualise your goal

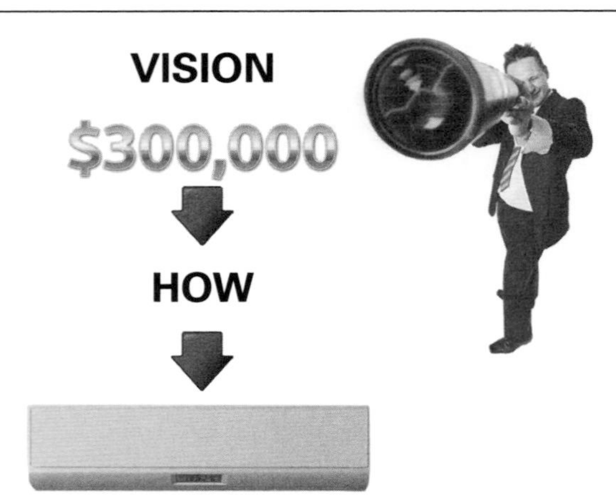

$3,000 Profit from each Sale
<u>$300,000</u> = 100 sales needed per year

Work 48 weeks a year

100/48 weeks ➡ 2.08 Sales per Week

HOW MANY LEADS FOR A SALE ? **3**

HOW MANY LEADS PER WEEK NEEDED FOR 2.08 SALES?
(2.08*3) 6.24

We will round up to 7 leads a week!

This formula will guarantee your desired result

If you're working 6 days a week for the next 12 months and you are focused on your goal, then of course you're going to be able to achieve it.

So, to have the things that you want in life all you need to do is create a lead generation system that delivers 7 leads a week, that will create 2.08 sales, that will create $300,000 in profit for you and that will be the income you need to get your house, your car, your boat and whatever other things you decided on with your why list.

Have you worked out that this isn't luck. It is not because you're some blessed individual. It's simply because you decided to take control of your destiny and say, "Damn it, I will do whatever it takes to create my lead generation system because that means that I'm going to earn my $300,000 over the next 12 months and I'll be able to have the things that I really want in life and I'll be able to provide for my family and my community the way that I want to."

It doesn't get much simpler than that. Do you have the courage to commit to working out your plan and knowing what you need to do to achieve it and then do whatever it takes to get to the finishing line? When you commit to it, you will find that the challenge is not that hard. The real secret here, the real inconvenient truth, is to decide to get serious about what you want in life and understand that you have as much right to the good things in life as the next person.

INCONVENIENT TRUTH

Step one: Fill out the table at the back of the book and decide on the goals and the things that you really want to have.

Step two: Work out what sort of income you're going to require to have those things in life.

Step three: Reverse engineer your goal so that you know just what has to happen, how many leads you need to get in, how many sales you need to make to achieve your goal and then create that action plan for yourself.

CHAPTER 4

Magic Formula For Creating A Multi-Million Dollar Business

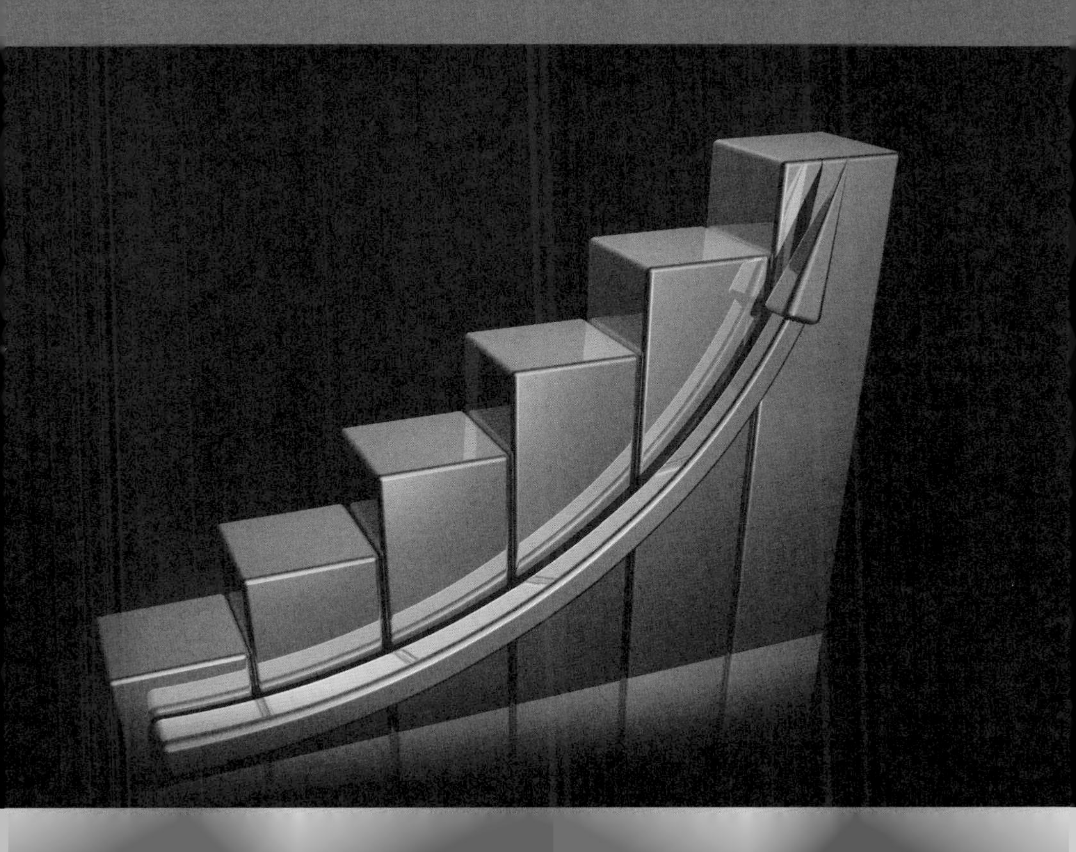

CHAPTER 4

Magic Formula For Creating A Multi-Million Dollar Business

In this chapter I am going to explain how you can find the perfect business to suit you and the formula that never fails when it comes to creating the right future for yourself. Up until now I've asked you to have a pretty hard look at your life and your world. If you've been in business for 5 to 7 years and you're not a millionaire already, then you're probably doing something wrong. Trust me, a million dollars doesn't get you too much in this day and age; it gets you a very average house in Sydney.

If that's your reality and you're ready to change things, then this chapter will probably reveal some glaring and inconvenient truths about why you may not be making the progress that you're wanting to in your business. So far we've looked at your background and learnt how your belief systems may be flawed, why you are in the world that you live in, taken a really honest look at what you want out of life and built up the courage to put it down on paper and say, "You know what? I really do deserve the good things in life."

You've said, "This is what I want in life and I have as much right to these things as anybody else," and then you've reverse engineered it so that you have the beginning of a plan to achieve those things that you are committed to.

Now, I don't have much tolerance for 'gunna' (I am going to do this) or 'roundtuit' (When I get around to it) people. In my world, if I want something I will go out and I will get it. That should be your experience as well. If you're serious about something, then don't let anything or anyone stop you from getting what you want. For that reason, I want to share this very powerful formula with you but before I explain the formula, I want to give you a real life example of how it plays out and why some people who have been in business for a long time may not be where they expected to be financially.

Let's take the business of a taxi driver for example. I happen to know this industry very well because I used to own a taxi plate in Sydney many years ago. I have a soft spot for taxi drivers because they're very hard workers and they don't get rewarded for the effort they put in. This is the story of a journey I took not that long ago when I hopped into a taxi with a very happy and pleasant Indian taxi driver.

When I take a taxi I always ask the driver how business is. Some of them tell me and some of them are guarded but most of them are very open about life and tell you what's going on in their world. This very affable Indian said, "Oh, life's very good. Really enjoying it. Working very hard. Love being here in Australia. So happy to be here."

"That's great," I said. "Do you enjoy driving a taxi?" He says, "Yes, this is a great business. I love it so much." I asked, "Why is it a great business?" He replied, "Well, you get to work for yourself and you meet lots of interesting people. You get to make the money that you want to make. You don't have anybody telling you what you must do. You get to choose how to work during the day; how hard or how slow you want to work." I said, "Oh, that's good."

We'll just call the driver Raj, so I said to him, "Tell me, Raj, how much money do you make driving a taxi?" He says, "Oh, most days I make $150." I said, "Really? How many hours do you work to generate that amount of money?" He said, "I work 12 hours a day. I start in the morning at 3:00am and I finish at 3:00pm in the afternoon. Then I give the car to another driver and I pay the lease for my taxi."

I said, "If you're getting $150 a day, how many days a week do you work?" He told me he works 6 days a week. He also told me he has a second job working as a cleaner for a company on Sundays. Raj works seven days a week. When somebody's working that hard I generally figure that they're saving for something so I asked Raj, "Tell me, Raj, are you really working 7 days a week and 12 hours a day? Why?"

Raj said, "I'm saving for a house." I said, "Okay, fantastic. Good on you. How close are you to that dream? I guess you're saving for a deposit. Is that right?" He said, "Yes, I am." "Raj, how long have you been saving for this house?"

He says, "Five years now, and I nearly have enough for a deposit." I said, "Okay Raj, I'm just curious because I do this for a living. I help people in business. Tell me, how much deposit have you saved up in those five years?" He says, "Oh, I have $30,000 now and I nearly have enough to get my house."

Raj could probably only afford a house for around $300,000 to $350,000. My point with this story is that Raj is leasing a taxi, he's making basically $150 a day and he's got to pay his tax out of that. Over five years he's managed to save $30,000. Even working seven days a week, it's taken a long time to finally get enough money for a deposit on a house.

This business has really prevented him from achieving what he wants, which isn't driving a taxi. He really wants to buy a house and he's trying to do the right thing by working hard to provide for his family. But is Raj doing things the smartest way? Sure, he is working hard. He is putting his head down and his backside up trying to get ahead in life. Raj is very happy in his environment, in his reality and he is very happy with his progress but here's the thing, Raj will eventually buy his house but he will then be in debt for the next 30 years. He was probably 35 when I chatted to him, which means that he will pay off his house at the age of 65 with maybe one or two trips back to India, if he is lucky, and that will be the life that he leads; working 80 hours a week and having no time for his family.

Now that's fine because he's happy in that world and that's the world that he wants to live in but what he doesn't know is that with the same effort and a commitment to study, he could be making $300 or $500 per hour instead of $12 per hour. He just needs to change his business vehicle. My question to you is this, if Raj knew another world, a world in which he could achieve the same thing in 5 years instead of 30 or 40 years, do you think that he might be wise enough to take that path and get to that end result quicker? Well, I can't answer for Raj but I think that most people would say yes.

Let's see where the flaw is in this because Raj is working harder than most people I know but his progress to getting the things that he wants in life is a lot slower than most people I know. Why? Number one is that he's swapping time for money. He can only earn X amount of money and only when somebody is in his taxi. Even if he was booked all day, he can only earn up to a certain amount of money. That's not a good thing. So, there is no leverage in this model.

Now, another thing to add to Raj's woes is that today's technology is decimating his industry. If he's wise, he will find another industry to get into because for years now, Google has had a car that drives around without a person in it and it can navigate the streets of California effortlessly, hence there is no need to have a driver. Does that mean that in the future there will not be a need for taxis? I would say that there is a good chance of it happening. What's even scarier is that these driverless cars will not have accidents, so there will be no smash repairers and if there are no accidents, what will happen to the insurance companies? And if we have driverless cars, there will be no speeding fines, so the government will not be able to get revenue from drivers and claim they are only doing it to save lives. (I'm afraid I got 2 speeding fines last week, so am slightly jaundiced).

There is also some very convenient technology called Uber. Even though I love taxi drivers (as I've mentioned previously) I use Uber a lot because I instantly know how far away my ride is. I don't have to worry about paying for the fare after I get out of the cab because it's all in my account. More and more people are using Uber, which means fewer people are using taxis and that obviously upsets the taxi drivers.

Now the taxi drivers and the government will fight it but they will lose because the masses will demand the convenience of Uber. As much as governments will be unhappy because they won't get their taxes from the sale of taxi plates and taxi drivers will be unhappy because the plates that were once worth $500,000, yes $500,000 for a taxi plate in Sydney, are now worth $200,000 and dropping like a sinker and they can't find buyers for the taxi plates so the transport industry is on the verge of a major upheaval.

With these scenarios happening, do you think that Raj's business model is a good one?

Some of you may feel sorry for Raj but let's look at your business - it is time for another inconvenient truth. Do any of these scenarios ring true about your business model? Probably, although not quite as painfully but just like the taxi driver, many of you are not getting to your financial destination because you have blockages. You have flaws in your magic business formula that you need to fix before time runs out on you and you are on the financial scrap heap like many Australians will be when they finish their working life.

According to a recent survey by REST, 86% of Australians will not be prepared for retirement and if you think the government is going to look after you, think again. Imagine living on $26,000 a year!

Now here's the magic formula for a business. Before you go into any business you need to ensure that these five things have had their boxes ticked:

1. Maths in the business
2. Psychology
3. Lifestyle
4. Sunrise
5. Minus sunset

Equals spectacular business.

Maths + psychology + lifestyle + sunrise - sunset = Great Business

Maths

What does that formula have to do with a successful business? Before I look at any business opportunity, the very first thing that I look at is the margins in the business. I've been responsible for building many multi-million dollar websites in my time and I have had a very successful career doing that, making myself and other people quite wealthy by having a successful presence online. With that being said, many of the individuals out there now think they have a successful online business. They proudly say to their friends, "Wow, I turned over a million dollars this year," and it may actually impress some people who are not streetsmart but all experienced business owners know that is not the turnover that is important, it is the profit that is left over at the end of the day. Unfortunately for many of these online businesses, they only have a mark-up of between 10% and 15%.

If a business that's online is doing a million dollars in turnover a year but they only have a 15% margin on what they're selling, then that means they've only got $150,000 to pay for everything.

Let's remember that you have internet costs, you have telephones, you have wages, you have distribution costs and you have insurances. Very often that million dollar a year online business that you hear about is lucky to net the owner of that business $40,000 or $50,000 a year.

This isn't just an opinion. I have worked with hundreds of business owners and taught thousands and these are facts. When I go into an organisation and look at the buying prospects I want to look at the maths in the business. 10% is not going to cut it.

I like looking at businesses that have decent margins of 60%, 70%, 100% and even 200% or more in them. The reason why you need these decent margins is because, especially in this day and age, if you don't have enough profit in what you're selling, you won't have the marketing dollars you need to be able to get your message out to the world to let them know just how good you are. And with people being slammed with at least 5,000 messages a day, you will more than likely fade into insignificance.

That's the first part of the formula. Is there good maths in the business? After you look at the maths, you've got to look at the psychology.

Psychology

The psychology of a business means that are there lots of individuals out there that want what you have. People think if they go out there and they build a better mousetrap that millions of people will go out there and buy that mouse trap. The sad truth is that most people already have a mousetrap and it will be difficult to convince them that yours is better. Look at the battle between VHS and BETA video (I am showing my age now). BETA was a far superior technology however, VHS had already grabbed a massive foothold and there was no shaking them.

The streetsmart way to approach your product creation is to work out the gap in the market where lots of people want something but there is no current solution for that something to fill that gap. What you will find most people doing is to approach their product offering in the opposite manner. Using me as an example, when I did my trade as an electrician, I went out into the world expecting that everybody wanted an electrician but I soon learned that it wasn't true. I had to be more refined than that. I had to look at the problems and the gaps that were there and then fill the gaps in the marketplace. It was not until I learned this secret that I started to make money.

Don't get a product and then try and sell it to a market. Have a look at the market first and make sure that there are a lot of people that want what you are thinking of providing. Then develop that product to suit what they want and provide it at a decent profit.

Streetsmart Hint: Do your best not to get involved in offering something that is a commodity. For example, don't open another Holden dealership where you're selling a six-cylinder Holden Commodore, exactly the same model as the dealer down the road, and try to convince somebody to buy it from you instead of them. The only thing that you can really base the sale on is price and you will lead a very sad life if that's the case, unless you can make your Commodore unique, something that your competitor cannot offer your client.

Sunrise or Sunset?

Now when you've looked at the maths and see that you've got a good margin and you look at the psychology and you see that there are a lot of people that want what you have, you then look at whether your business is a sunrise or a sunset business. I will explain this by telling you another story of a person that I tried to help in Albany many, many years ago. He had a video store. He called us up and asked us if we could assist him because his profits were diminishing. He'd been in video rentals for many, many years and made quite a bit of money out of it but for some reason that he couldn't work out, his profits were dwindling.

Well I went down to Albany. It was about a five hour drive to get there although I didn't know it at the time. When I got to Albany I realised that this business was in trouble, in was a sunset business. I had a chat with the owner, who we'll call Joe for the sake of this exercise.

I said, "Now Joe, I know you've been in business and you've been profitable for quite a while but here's the reality. There are people who are downloading latest release movies from the internet and they are not paying for them. I don't know how they do it. I don't understand it. I don't want to understand it because I don't think it's right but they are bragging to me about how they have just watched the latest

Hollywood blockbuster straight off the internet. If they are able to do that now, don't you think that other people are also going to learn how to download movies? If they can do that, why would they come to you and pay money for a video? They can just get it for free at home, without leaving their house."

Well Joe didn't like what I told him and said, "Oh rubbish. We'll be around. Everybody will want these videos." Sadly I did try one more time. I said, "Joe, if you would like me to help you I would like you to innovate because my son is now a mad gamer and he lives in front of the TV, playing bloody Xbox and Playstation and Call of Duty. It's like an addiction; he just won't remove himself from the screen. Why don't you transform your business into a gaming shop so that people can come and get video games from you?"

This was before EB Games and similar businesses became popular. Anyway, Joe listened to what I had to say and said thank you very much but I knew that would be the last I heard from him. Two years later I went back to Albany and sadly that store that had once been a thriving business was all closed up. Nobody was there and that was the end of Joe. I heard that Joe lost pretty much everything he had worked for all his life and ended up divorced. What was worse is that I believe he put a lot of the money that he made previously back into the business to try and keep it alive because at the time that I was talking to him, he was telling me he had to prop it up with the equity from his home.

Now there are hundreds of thousands of stories like Joe's out there. The thing that I want you to do is learn from Joe and not be a victim of change like he was. As much as you might be emotionally attached to your business, there is a sunrise period in a business and there is a sunset. You would not want to be involved in the film business now producing Kodak film for cameras. Why? Because digital decimated it and pretty well decimated Kodak. You would not want to be in the offset printing game now or, as I mentioned earlier, the limousine or taxi industry. They may have been good in their day but just like it says in the bible, there is a time to reap and a time to sow. Work out the season of your industry and be very honest in your appraisal.

That's the maths. Is it a good margin? The psychology - do lots of people want what you have? A sunrise business is one that is moving up. When Steve Jobs created the Apple iPhone, with all the functions of a smartphone, that was the time to get into the phone business. People wanted phones. Now that phones have largely become a commodity, it's time to look for the next opportunity. There's many of them out there.

LIFESTYLE

The last thing that I want you to be looking at when you're considering a business is lifestyle. When you're considering buying a business, think about whether you would have to be in that business seven days a week. Would you have to be open for weekend trading? Would you have to put in 12 hour days? Would the business have to have you in it for it to run or is it a business that runs under management, has strong and clear key performance indicators that you can easily manage and where you only need to go in one or two days a week to see how things are going? Is it a turnkey operation that is a license to print money?

That is the sort of business that I'd be urging you to look for. They do exist and there are quite a lot of them out there but most people don't think strategically. They think emotionally and say, "Wow, I'd really love to be doing this" but you don't get very wealthy by working in the business, you get wealthy by working on the business.

It's a very old cliché and probably every man and his dog says it but there's never a truer word said, and quite frankly, I see very few individuals do it! You must be the strategist and you must be the visionary and the leader, taking the business where you want it to go. Not being the mechanic in the business but turning the cogs of the organisation. When you add these together, the maths, plus the psychology, plus the sunrise business, minus the sunset business, plus the lifestyle you have an extremely powerful formula for choosing a successful business.

So, are you ready to look at your own business and apply this formula?

What is the maths like in your business? Have you got pretty poor maths in there?

With the psychology, is there still a hungry crowd desperate for what you have? Although there may be a lot of people who want what you have, are you a commodity which makes it very, very difficult to separate you from another individual that's selling what you have?

If you have ticked those two boxes let's look at the existing demand in your industry.

Are you in a sunrise or a sunset business? Has your market matured where it's reached its peak or has it plateaued or is it declining? Can you innovate? If not, can you evacuate?

Finally, does this business need to consume every minute of your life? Does it need to have you there 6 or 7 days a week, working 12 hours a day or can it be developed into a business that can largely run by itself?

I do not want you to misinterpret what I am teaching you here. When you start a business, it may take you 3 to 5 years of working very hard to build the foundations and create a turnkey operation and you could be working 6 or 7 days a week to develop the business to get it to that point.

My point here is that it must be a business that has the ability to be turned into a turnkey operation that can run without you. You must always have that end in mind if you want to create your multi-million dollar business. In fact, that is my model. I start a business, work very hard in it for 5-7 years, have it structured ready for sale, get a nice pay day, have a rest for 8 or 9 months and then move on to the next opportunity. **NEVER relax for longer than 12 months**. I was talking to Gerry Harvey a while ago and he said, "Ian, I never employ someone that has been out of the mix longer than a year. They go soft, their mind slows down and usually, they have not kept up with the times."

INCONVENIENT TRUTH

Some **TOUGH QUESTIONS** for you:

Do you have good maths in your business?

Do you have good psychology in your business?

Do you have a sunrise or a sunset business?

Can it have a great lifestyle attached to it?

If you have an ugly baby, what are you going to do about it?

CHAPTER 5

Building A Spectacular Team

CHAPTER 5

Building A Spectacular Team

The commonly held misconception is that the success of your business is because of you. I'm here to tell you that even though you are the driving force, the motivation and the inspiration for your organisation, the reality is that for you to have a real business, you're going to need help. That help comes from your team, the staff that you employ to help you achieve the vision that you have and the goal that you're setting out to accomplish. For many of you, that goal may be vague and fuzzy rather than clear and distinct and my guess is that 80% of you who are reading this book probably couldn't articulate why you are in business. If you stood up in front of your staff and said to them, "Guys, we're in business today because................" you would probably draw a blank with the rest of that sentence.

Every week I religiously have a staff meeting with my team and I share with them the success stories that we have accomplished for our members. I let them know how we are truly helping people achieve financial and lifestyle freedom in 3 to 5 years or less and how each and every one of them is responsible for helping make that happen. That's my vision. That's what spurs me on and everyone in my company knows that and if they don't share in that vision and they're only there for a paycheque, then they generally don't last too long in my company.

Your staff are not working with you purely because of the money. Some of them are but your staff are working with you for a number of reasons not related to money. Perhaps they believe in you, they believe in what you're trying to accomplish and they love the environment that they're in. In many surveys that have been done, the money that the staff members earn is a secondary consideration to the difference that they are making in what they are actually doing with their job, as strange as that may seem to some of you.

Maybe they want to learn skills to improve their talents and believe that you are the right person to learn from. Maybe they have an ulterior motive and want to learn your systems and processes and steal your clients from you. It is important that you understand what motivates your staff to help you succeed in your company. (The key word is help).

Here's the reality. If you don't have a great team around you, there will be serious ramifications to your success. The very best companies have the very best teams. The second best companies have the second best teams and the third best companies, they go out of business. How do I know that? Well, one reason is that Brian Tracy taught me this many years ago and another is that I had to learn this lesson from personal experience.

I want to take you back to the first large organisation that I built. It was called Marsh Air Conditioning. The reason why I managed to grow this organisation to be one of the largest in

New South Wales, and probably one of the largest domestic air conditioning companies in Australia, was simply because I had mastered the fine art of sales and marketing.

Little did I know at the time, that having a successful business relied on much, much more than just being able to make a sale and convert it. Anyway, when I started this organisation it started as many people's businesses do. I had a small team with two apprentices, a tradesman and a sales person. We were young and we were full of passion and we were having a really good time. There were six of us working there. Many times we would be working fourteen and fifteen hour days to get the job done but we did not mind, we were having a ball and it was fun putting the installations together.

Everybody loved what they were doing. We were always smiling and joking and I was part of the gang. I was helping the staff with the installation of the air conditioning systems and everybody felt that they were a nice tight family unit. Within 5 years it was one of the largest air conditioning companies in Australia and I had 60 staff working for me but my core team and I started to grow apart. After a while, one of my core team, my head sales person, felt that he didn't have to put in the same effort that he had initially. This particular sales person decided that he didn't have to justify the amount of work that he was doing each day and he felt that he didn't need to apprise me of the number of quotes he was doing or keep track of the sales and conversions.

Now, the only reason I started looking for these statistics was because I got a business coach in to start coaching me and he said, "Please tell me what your conversion rates are. Tell me how many leads you need to be able to get a sale? How effective is your sales team?"

Embarrassingly, I had no answers for him so I started putting those systems in place. But this particular sales person that had been with me for years got his knickers in a knot and I believe he felt that I did not trust him anymore, so he dug his heels in and decided he did not want to provide the details so that I could analyse his efforts.

This was a really interesting situation for me. I was thinking, "Who's the boss here? I'm the one paying you. You're not the one paying me." Quite interestingly, we butted heads. Anyway, I could not get him to play ball with me and so after five years of very loyal service and doing great work, even though it did go on a sliding trajectory in the last year and a half, we parted company and I sacked him. This individual really had an unpleasant parting with us. He destroyed the engine in the company car and he created hell for me, claiming psychological depression and a whole heap of other things that really milked the organisation and cost me a fortune in workers compensation.

What was worse was that the rest of my core team who initially thought the world of me, calling me the very best boss in the world, (they actually bought me number plates for my car and really thought of me as a sort of father figure), thought that my sales person was hard done by because I expected him to explain what he was doing in the organisation during the day and to provide reports for me. At that stage the culture of the company started to go bad.

That was the turning point in my company. A cancer set into the organisation and a rot started to develop. I could sense it. I didn't want to admit it but the rot started to permeate right throughout the whole organisation because the staff believed the stories my salesperson had told them.

They didn't know the whole story of course. They didn't know that the salesperson that I sacked wasn't doing the work expected of him. They just believed the untruths that their mate used to justify his case, making me out to be some kind of boss from hell.

Essentially, I had a mutiny on my hands but I tried not to admit it. I put blinkers on my eyes but it came to a head quite dramatically because instead of making a nice profit every month and living the life of an entrepreneur with a successful business, I started making some serious losses every month, and I mean really big losses. Being a sales and marketing guy, I figured the way to fix that was to make more sales, so I had my head down and my bum up and was making more and more sales and bringing more and more money in but sure enough, I was losing more and more out the back end and wondering what the hell was going on.

What occurred next absolutely shocked me and quite honestly broke my heart. One electrician who was working for me decided to do the wrong thing by his wife and he got caught cheating on her. Well, hell hath no fury like a woman scorned. Sure enough, the wife got on the phone to us and told us that her husband was cheating on her and so she felt compelled to dob him in. Her husband had been stealing materials from me and she could not live with that thought any more.

Obviously, I sent one of my supervisors out to check on the story the wife was telling us and this is when reality set in for me.

My supervisor rang me and he was stammering on the end of the phone. He was saying "B-B-B Boss, you gotta see this."

I would like you to visualise this. At the time I was doing about a million dollars a month in sales. If you've ever seen a large farm shed, I mean the huge ones that the big farmers put their massive combine harvesters in, they're gigantic. If you could picture a farm shed like that packed solid, top to bottom, with air conditioning ducts, with air conditioning fan coils, with copper, electrical cable, air conditioning condensers and at least a million dollars or more worth of stock in there, then you would have an indication of the sort of theft that was going on in my company.

Sadly, I'm not Robinson Crusoe here. Since I have been consulting, I have come across many other entrepreneurs who have suffered a very similar fate to me. I have x-ray vision now and can spot the symptoms very quickly but let me get back to my story.

We saw all of this material in this person's shed and we rang the police but between the time that she dobbed in her husband and when the police turned up from Blacktown Police Station six hours later, the wife had had a change of heart and rang her husband. She said, "Listen, this is what I've done, honey," so that by the time the police arrived the shed had been completely emptied, bar a tiny pile of material left in the back corner of the shed and a big pantechnicon was driving off into the distance, probably with the last load of their ill-gotten gains.

Understand the emotional trauma that I was going through. All the profits that I should have been making in my company had disappeared and they had gone off and been shared among a number of the staff in my organisation. I was employing around sixty people at the time. I was sitting there in the Blacktown Police Station feeling sorry for myself and wanting to go after those individuals and do what I could to recoup what had been taken.

The detective came and sat down beside me and said, "Ian, it's like this. You can spend your time and years in the courts trying to chase these guys. They haven't got any money behind them anyway. They're practically giving away your gear for nothing. You could chase them and have them in the courts and spend a fortune trying to get recompense or you can just let this go and move on with your life and forget this incident ever happened. It's your choice but I've been in this business a long time and seen similar things happen to other business owners and I'm telling you, you're far better off just moving on with your life."

So, I actually took his advice and decided to let it go. I then declared bankruptcy because not only had they stolen a lot of material from me, they had also stolen a lot of labour from me in terms of taking three times longer to do a job, having call-backs and doing really poor work. The reality was that it crippled my organisation.

Obviously, I learned some inconvenient truths from that experience and I'll tell you, my life hinged on a paper thin choice at that time because, as you can imagine, I'd gone from being a multi-millionaire to being bankrupt and my sense of worth was non-existent. In fact, I felt completely worthless. If it wasn't for a conversation that I had with a mentor of mine, I could very well be lying on the beach at Byron Bay drinking away every brain cell I possess.

I want you to consider how you would feel if one day you are able to buy your wife anything she desires, buy cars for your friends and send family overseas on lovely holidays and the next minute wondering how you're going to put food on the table, get your children to school and buy shoes for them. It's a pretty harrowing experience. In fact, a lot of the motivation for me to do what I do today comes because I would never wish that experience on anybody. In fact, I believe it's better if you're poor and you've never been wealthy because then you don't know what you're missing out on but once you've been poor and you become wealthy and then you become poor again, you have a very healthy respect for being financially secure.

Some inconvenient truths that I learned from this process and that I want to share with you are the following:

Do you have an organisational chart in your business? Even if you're a one man band, you should always have a vision of what your business will look like in 12 months, 2 years, 5 years and in the future and understand the staff that you will need to have to fulfil those roles e.g. the accountant for the accounts division, the sales manager for the sales division and the marketing manager for your marketing. You need to be serious and say, "If I want a real company, I'm going to need these people one day," and you need to live towards that.

Do I have a clear role and responsibility for each of my staff members and do they actually know how to fulfil their roles? Have I trained them thoroughly on how to do what I expect them to do or have I just thrown them into that position and let them be trained by the existing staff with no rhyme or reason or structure to the end result? Do I have tests so that I know that they've been trained and actually know how to do their job? Have you had them sign off to say, "This is how I will do my job. I understand my expectations and I believe that I can fulfil them." Then on top of that, have you developed and created measuring systems and key performance indicators for your staff so that you can measure how effective they are and if they are doing their job properly?

Jack Welsh was the CEO of General Electric and he had it right. Essentially, in your company, 20% of your staff will be top performers. You should look after these individuals like family. You should be showering them with gifts and praise and telling them just how wonderful they are. You will also have 70% of individuals who are okay. They're doing their job but they are nothing to write home about. Your future 20% of top performers will come from this 70% so you need to consistently nurture them and train them because you don't want to lose the 70% but you need to work out how to help them move up to the top 20%.

Then, finally, you've got the bottom 10% of your company, the people who don't perform, no matter what you do to try and help them. There's only one thing you can do with that 10%, as much as you may find it distasteful, you need to free them up for other opportunities because if you leave that 10% in your organisation, they will bring down the standard of the rest of your company and it can create a cancer in your organisation. As I've just explained in my story, it can destroy you and your dream if you let it. You need to make sure that you protect the culture of your organisation and that the people who are in your company should be there and if you have even the slightest hesitation, then follow your instincts and act on your intuition. Do not be scared about what it may cost to remove that person because keeping them there will cost you 10 times more!!!

I understand that some of you may think you can't ever sack that person because you wonder how you will find somebody else. I have worked in hundreds of industries and I have had that same question from many owners, worried that they are not going to be able to replace the person. Believe me when I say that that little voice is telling you a lot of hogwash and nine times out of ten, the person that replaces the one that's being removed, is three or four times better at the role than the person that they replaced.

Another scenario that is very common is when a staff member has been with you for a long time. They're part of the furniture. I know they're not going to like it if you ask them to start doing things differently and justifying their position. What will you do if the staff member quits? What happens if they get upset with you?

It is normal to have those thoughts but you can't afford to let those emotions rule your decisions. You need to do what is right in your heart. You need to act on what you believe as the leader of your organisation or else you're not leading your company, rather, the staff are leading you. Unfortunately, this is an occurrence that I see on a daily basis. Please face this inconvenient truth. Ask yourself, knowing what you know now, would you reemploy that person again? If the answer is no, then it's time to free them up for other opportunities.

INCONVENIENT TRUTH

Do you have an organisational chart?

Do you have individual roles and responsibilities for your staff members?

Do you have a structured training process when new staff come on?

Do you have a culture in your business?

Is it a good one?

Do you reward and recognise your top staff?

Knowing what you now know, is there any staff member that you would not employ again?

If there is, what are you going to do about it?

CHAPTER 6

Do You Have A Job Or A Business?

CHAPTER 6

Do You Have A Job Or A Business?

You know, before I started understanding how a business should run, my life was pretty crazy!

Let me tell you what my life was like with Marsh Air Conditioning before I knew any better.

It pretty well started out like this. I would wake up at 4:00am every morning, go into the office, plan all the work for the guys, try to do all the invoicing, look at any quotes that needed doing and do as much preparation for the day as I could before everyone else got to work. Then the day would start and I would answer questions asked by the staff left, right and centre. Many times the same question would be asked over and over and over again. Some of the questions were so silly that I don't know how the people asking them had graduated from primary school, let alone high school. Then after I got the staff busy in the morning I would be out on the road doing quotes for clients and bringing in sales with my salesperson. While I was driving along on the road, I hardly ever stopped for a minute in between quotes. Sometimes I'd duck into McDonald's and grab something via the drive through and be back on the road driving the car with my knees while I was talking on the phone with my left hand and simultaneously eating a Big Mac with my right. As a result, I started to develop a belly the size of Tasmania. (Still trying to lose it, damn it!)

I'd keep going like a mad dog and my last quote would end at around 8:00pm. I'd stumble through the door around about 9:00pm or 10:00pm that evening, look in on my son and daughter asleep, mumble something to my long suffering wife and repeat the process the next day.

Now, that story is how I started to grow Marsh Air Conditioning and it was like that for at least three years. As I said to you earlier, I mastered the art of sales and marketing; which I still maintain are the most important skills to master. What I hadn't mastered were the other business skills that are critical to keeping the ship afloat. I thought that if I could just get more sales then all my problems would be over. How wrong I was. The business that I had, even though it was making incredible amounts of money, didn't really give me the perfect life that I dreamed of. The amount of time I got to spend with my children or build my relationship with my family was pretty much zero. I worked non-stop, seven days a week. Having said that, the money was great and the ego was great and I was going at a million miles an hour. I didn't know any better.

Until, as I told you in an earlier story, it all came to a screaming halt. In many ways it was one of the best things that could have happened to me. You will find that when life hands you what you believe is the biggest crisis in your life or the biggest obstacle and you smash through it and come through the other side, there's such personal growth. This, in turn, expands your world and exposes you to the new realities that exist out there but the crisis had to happen or you would not have changed and grown. Before you break through the catastrophes that occur in your life, you think that the world has ended and it's not worth moving forward but for those few who do keep moving forward and don't give up, you find that when you push through, incredible things happen on the other side. That's exactly what happened to me because even though I became bankrupt with my first company, I went on to grow four other multi-million dollar organisations.

Many people may be justified in giving up, as I nearly did, but the 20% that don't give up reap the rewards that are due to them. It is a universal law that "you get what you give." If you give the problem everything you've got, then you will get back multiples of what you have given.

So what does your business look like? Can you relate to my story in any way? Does it ring some bells for you? Let's just do a quick test shall we and see if you have a business or a job.

- Can you leave your company for six weeks at a time and come back to a smooth running organisation? Yes or no?

- Can your business operate if you are only there two days a week, yes or no?

- Is your business paying you the income you desire while still making a decent profit for the company? Yes or no?

- Can your staff solve 80% of the issues that occur in the business on a day to day basis? Yes or no?

- Do you think that other people might love to own your business or are they thinking, "Thank God that I'm not in his shoes?" Yes or no?

Well, if you answered yes to at least four out of these five questions, congratulations, because you're part of the 5% of company owners that actually have a business and not a job.

But if you're one of the 80% of readers who answered no, then I'm going to ask you another question. When do you want to start answering yes to these questions? When you started out in business, I'm sure you had goals and dreams and visions of what your business would be like. How's that working for you?

If you aren't happy with how you scored in that test, when are YOU going to change things?

You can actually start answering yes to the above questions immediately if you want to. All you need to do to start answering yes to the questions is simply DECIDE that that's how your business is going to be. That is what you are going to create for your organisation. You are going to have this life and this business that you've always wanted and you are going to create the plans, the actions, THE PEOPLE and the strategies NECESSARY to make it a reality.

All you need to do is believe that it's possible. Once you believe that it's possible and you put your passion behind that belief, then you create a plan to actually make it a reality. All you need to do then is work the plan and not give up, no matter how tough it is. If this was a walk in the park, everybody would be multi-millionaires but once again, the universal law kicks in. Not everyone is willing to do what it takes to become a successful entrepreneur and have a business that can run without you. This is for those people who are willing to roll up their sleeves, grasp that dream and do whatever it takes to make it happen. Are you that person?

Well then, it is time to understand what you actually get paid for as the business owner.

As a business owner, many people think that you should be in the organisation and you should be solving everybody's problems and that when they come to you, you're the genius that can make the problem go away. **For a lot of business owners, that's really their sense of worth. That gives them a sense of being**, of why they're the boss - because they have this ability to solve problems. It gives them a kind of adrenaline rush, like a drug!

But does that really make sense? Do you want a business that's full of problems all the time or would you like a business that has the occasional challenge but largely runs fairly smoothly and without massive stress every day?

Do you want a business that provides you with a lifestyle that you would like to be accustomed to? Obviously, most people would like the latter. After you get over this need to be great and solve everybody else's problems, what you should be doing is looking at what you really get paid for in the organisation and trust me, it is not being the person that everybody comes to, to solve their problems.

As the business owner, you need to be the person that creates the vision and ensures that all of the staff know why you open your doors. They know the purpose that they have in coming to work. They know what their part in that big purpose is and they're proud to be working for an organisation that achieves that goal.

As the owner of the company you need to lead your team and inspire them to work towards your vision. So, you need to build the right team to fulfil your vision. You need to ensure that you give your team the right resources, the right training and the right guidance to achieve their goals and you then need to monitor the results that your team are getting and make adjustments as necessary. That is your role as the owner. It is not for you to be involved in the actual doing of the work. It is not for you to be doing the paperwork and the bookwork. If you're filling that type of role in the company then there is a good chance you are actually creating a blockage in your organisation, whether you realise it or not, and costing yourself a lot of money in the process.

In fact, this was another big revelation in my ability to grow multi-million dollar companies. It was a key turning point that took me from being a tactician to being a strategist, the result of which was to start making serious money in my company.

Let me show you what I mean. When I was in air conditioning, if I was installing an air conditioner with my team, there wouldn't be many challenges and the owner would be happy with the job because I'd make sure we'd go above and beyond to look after them and the stress levels would be low because I controlled everything.

Life would be pretty predictable but I had a limit to what I could do. At most, if I was on the tools, I could only install three ducted systems a week. That would be a bit of a challenge because it would cap my income. For me to earn the sort of money that I wanted to earn in my business I needed to make a lot more money than the $4,500 a week, which is what my gross profit would have been. Then I realised that if I had my team doing the job instead of me, I could spend my time working out ways to do 20 jobs a week rather than 3 jobs a week and I could focus on the sales and marketing and the operation of the company while they focussed on doing the installations. Instead of me doing 3 jobs a week, I would have massive leverage and be able to make incredible money and achieve my vision and the goals that I wanted to achieve.

So, the way that I transitioned from being on the tools was that I started taking every Friday afternoon off. I decided that no matter what, come hell or high water, I'm going to let the company know that on Friday afternoon I've got a very important meeting with someone and I will not be at work from 12:00pm onwards. Then I went off to a quiet environment and turned off my phone so I was not contactable and I spent that half a day strategising on sales and marketing ideas to improve the results for my company. After about two months of doing that the sales were increasing, the business was surviving and I realised that they could handle being without me for half a day. Then I wondered how they'd handle being without me for a full day if I spent the whole day working on sales and marketing strategies. Sure enough, I started taking every Friday off and I'd be working on my ideas and strategies and relationships and joint ventures and seeing key clients. Once again, my business was still there even though I was only there four days a week and not five. I thought, 'Wow! This is pretty good.'

I wonder if my company could still operate, even though I know all my clients want to deal with me, if I put a general manager in. Would he be able to do what I do and run the company instead of me? So I found a general manager and put him in place and let him do what he did best, which was run the company.

Here is an important side note, another inconvenient truth:

Many business owners make the decision to bring in a general manager when they have been in business for 3 to 5 years and they've been working their tail off. Naturally, they are pretty exhausted by the time they get the business to a point where they can bring a general manager in. It's making money and profits are good but the business owner is emotionally and physically worn out and when he finds somebody with half a brain and thinks that they might be able to do the job, the business owner often says, "Here's the business, I want you to run it," rather than transition the person into the role and give the person divisions of the company to manage to prove themselves. They say, "You do everything and I'm going to go off and have a holiday," and they haphazardly check on a few things here and there.

They might even disappear and not have much to do with the business and let the GM run the company. Unfortunately, time and time and time again, when that business owner realises that profits are disappearing and sales are dropping and the best people are leaving, they come back and start looking closely at what is going on and more often than not they find that the business is in crisis and there's not enough money in the bank and all the key clients have left them. The business is failing. Why has this occurred?

Well, it's because rather than the business owner delegating tasks to a general manager they have abdicated their post and didn't closely monitor the results the general manager was getting or hold him accountable for them.

My advice here is that your strategic goal should be to get the business to a point where you can systematically remove yourself for a few hours a week to begin with. Then half a day and then a day, then maybe two days a week until you get to the point where you can leave a general manager to run the place instead of you but don't let him manage the whole organisation. You need to say okay, so you're the general manager and you're on a six month probation. I'm going to give you this division to look after, now let me see how well you manage to make it perform. (This could be 25% of the workload that the owner has on their plate.) Then observe them managing that division. All companies have core divisions in them like accounting, sales, marketing, logistics and customer service. They're pretty standard divisions in any organisation. So delegate one or two of those divisions to him over time. You can start taking things a bit easier but you can also closely monitor what that person is looking after and see how well they are performing in that area.

And when they perform well in that area then give them the next part and the next part but I urge you, do not abdicate the role of general manager to an individual just because you're exhausted and you think you need a break. If you do, the results will be catastrophic.

INCONVENIENT TRUTH

Here are some inconvenient truth questions for you.

Do you have a business or a job?

When are you going to decide to create a business?

When are you going to create a plan to develop this business?

Who will be the mentor that will guide you in transforming your job into a business?

CHAPTER 7

The Four Letter Word That Is Responsible for Why 92.5% Of Business Owners Never Achieve More Than A Million Dollars In Turnover

CHAPTER 7

The Four Letter Word That Is Responsible for Why 92.5% Of Business Owners Never Achieve More Than A Million Dollars In Turnover

I now want to talk about the four-letter word that is responsible for 92.5% of businesses never doing more than a million dollars in turnover. I have worked with thousands of businesses, talked to tens of thousands of people and witnessed what I believe is the biggest barrier to success in existence. Nothing surpasses this four-letter word and nothing causes more anxiety, more depression or more angst than this horrible word that I'm about to reveal to you but before I reveal it, I want to tell you a story about how I broke through the threshold of that dreaded million dollar turnover and went on to build each of my companies into multi-million dollar organisations.

Let's rewind back to a naïve electrician trying to make a dollar and starting to learn and understand the immense power that an organisation can have once they master the art of sales and marketing. Yes, that individual is me many, many years ago and I did become an avid student of sales and marketing and I did hone and perfect skills in those areas.

I am also glad I focussed on those skills because the fact is, in all the years that I've been consulting, by far the biggest reason why businesses fail is the owner's inability to attract, convert and keep a client. In other words, they don't have a reliable, predictable, affordable lead generation system.

I will share with you how to create one those fairly soon but I need to address this horrible four-letter word and how it applied to me. I started to kick some goals and win more than my fair share of quotations once I became a master of sales. I would go out and see individuals and I would convert 82% of the qualified prospects that I would meet. This was no accident; it was simply because I focused on studying the art of sales and marketing. I wonder - what would your business be like with a conversion rate at that level?

At the time, when I became very good at sales and marketing, my business was stuck at a plateau of $900,000 per annum for nearly two years. During that time, I was working my little derriere off, trying to make my business more successful. I knew that I wanted to get bigger and I knew that I wanted to make more money and yet I was staying where I was. I would do my level best to get as many leads as I could and I'd be out there quoting until all hours of the night and converting sales.

No matter what I did, I was trapped at this $900,000 level until an individual knocked on my door and asked me if he could work for me as my salesperson. This individual's name was Mike and when he knocked on my door he actually forced me to break through one of my inconvenient mental barriers. The simple idea of trusting another individual to make sales for me and the fear of trying to find an additional $70,000 to pay a salesperson to do sales instead of me doing all the sales and installations and bookwork was a very daunting thought. In fact, it scared the willies out of me and I was breaking into a cold sweat for nearly two weeks just thinking about having the salesperson join my team. Why was it that I delayed making the decision to employ an additional salesperson in my business? I already had more leads than I could effectively deal with and I was running around like a mad dog trying to keep up and not looking after all of the enquiries the way that I should have.

Logic told me that I could put this individual on and if I did, well then I would have more sales and that would mean more money but I had to have an honest conversation with myself. That for me to grow and to become one of the largest air conditioning companies in New South Wales, I would need to put my trust in other individuals and allow them to take responsibilities off my shoulders. The scariest thoughts that were going through my head before I made the decision to put this salesperson on were, "What if he can't sell? Where am I going to find the extra money? What if he's not as good as I am? Do I want more staff?" But really, even though these questions going through my mind were somewhat valid, the real question that I had to face, the real issue that I had to confront was, "Ian, are you really serious about becoming successful in business or are you just playing games and mucking around the edges?"

If we take this person on it means more sales, which means more staff, which means more vans, which means this will become a real business and won't just be Ian Marsh responsible for almost everything. This will be the start of something big. I hadn't realised that even though I thought I was doing everything I could to become successful in my business; I was actually scared of my success. I was scared of having too many sales, so I was scared of getting too much work. I was scared of being responsible for other people and providing work to keep them busy. What was occurring was that I was sabotaging my success and delaying my financial future simply because of fear. Yes, that four-letter word F.E.A.R.

Again, I need to reinforce this fact! You are where you are in life because of the decisions and choices that you make. Quite honestly, the biggest inconvenient truth of all is fear. You are afraid of something. In fact, we all are but until you recognise that and until you confront and are willing to acknowledge it, embrace it and overcome it, your fear will prevent you from achieving what you truly want in life.

If I had decided not to put that salesperson on, I never would have achieved the growth that I did.

This meant I would have been trapped like many tradesmen today, in a feast or famine cycle where I would get really busy with work, stop my lead generation, ignore clients so that I could install the sales that I got, then, when the work ran out, go to the market again, try to get more leads, get busy, ignore the other leads coming in because I am busy installing until the work runs out and the cycle continues. Does this sound familiar to anyone? Well, if you are not happy with that cycle, don't you think it is time to change?

Now, to prove my point, in the 12 months after putting Mike on, the income went from $900,000 to $1.8 million. In the following 12 months, I went from $1.8 million to just shy of $4 million. In the 12 months after that I went from $4 million to $9 million and in the next 12 months, I went from $9 million to $12 million in turnover. Can you see how just one tiny thought process in your mind can be responsible for massive success in your life? Just a very small change in belief systems, that, 'Hey, I don't need to do all the work. Yes, if I put a person on, I will be able to find enough business to be able to keep them busy. Yes, they'll be able to help me grow my organisation and take it where I need it to go.'

That very act of me confronting my fear and taking a leaf out of Richard Branson's book saying, "Screw it, let's do it," changed me from being a glorified technician in my air conditioning business to becoming one of the most successful companies in New South Wales. So my question to you is, do you have some hidden fears that you are not confronting? By the way, the answer is yes! I know this for a fact. If you are not where you want to be, there is some fear inside you that is preventing you from taking what you want in life. Is it the fear of success? Is it the fear of having too many staff and having to provide for them? Is it the fear of all the trouble that can come along with staff?

Whatever the fear is, this four letter word has stopped more individuals living the life that they deserve than any other thing I have ever witnessed. In my business school, I coach hundreds of business owners every year and without exception, I see this four letter word pop up over and over and over again.

A perfect example of this four letter word happened just recently when I was training my business advisers in their 1 day intensive training. I was preparing the material that I was going to teach them on the day and one throwaway line that I got from one of my advisers really put a bee in my bonnet.

You see, as a business consultant, my team are lucky enough to have what I believe is the perfect business vehicle. It ticks every box of my magic formula. It has incredible maths. It has wonderful psychology. It is a sunrise business. There are so many business owners that need assistance and it has the perfect lifestyle too. There are practically no overheads involved with it and hardly any staff are involved. In all honesty, I've never seen a simpler or more lucrative business model than in the world of business consulting.

Anyway, as I was preparing for this day of intensive training with my advisers, I was having a conversation with one of them and I asked, "How are things going?" The adviser replied, "It's going great. I'm really happy. I have my stationery, I have my book, I purchased my CRM, I have set up my office and I have decided on my USP so I guess I should be ready to get going soon." Now, this adviser had been in my environment for around 4 months but he hadn't got a client yet. By rights, he should have had 6 clients by then and be on at least $300,000pa. Now the adviser was still happy but the reality was that he was making every excuse not to start doing the things that would make him money, which was to get a client!

Anyway, it really set the cat among the pigeons because I got quite aggravated. I know that you can go out and you can get a client within 24 hours if you're serious in your business. Yet many individuals will take 3 months, 6 months or even 12 months before they actually get a client. Having said that, many of my advisers get a client within a short time of finishing their training, the record being 5 days.

At that moment, rather than spending a whole day teaching them more skills and giving them more strategies and teaching them more tactics on how to be a better business consultant, I issued a challenge. It was quite funny I have to admit. My business advisers had gathered for a training day, books and pens at the ready and I said to them, "Ladies and gentlemen, get ready. We're having a challenge today. You're going to go into Sydney and you are going to get expressions of interest from business owners who need help with their business. No ifs, buts or maybes, you are going to go out there and you are going to approach them. The person who comes back with the most expressions of interest is going to win $500." Well, you should have seen their faces drop. The blood went out of their skin, they went deathly pale and a look of panic started to develop around the room. "What? You mean we actually have to get out there and talk to business owners?" "Well, yes guys, isn't that why you became business advisers?"

I sent them out there and they had 4 hours to achieve their mission. When they returned they had 53 expressions of interests from business owners who said, "Hey, I actually do need help with my business." Now, if you translate that with the most conservative conversation rate that we have in our company, it works out to around $3 million worth of business in 4 hours. Quite impressive, right? Yet the same individuals had been waiting 3 months, 4 months or 6 months before they even started to get a lead.

As I said earlier, a lot of my advisers actually get clients within a few days of finishing their training. I wanted to help all of the advisers in there realise what their true potential was and what they're truly capable of because in the world of business consulting, you can easily earn $500 to $1,000,000 a year without breaking a sweat but you have to be serious. Now, I do want to stress that cold calling is the last strategy I want any of you using in your business as I much prefer prospects seeking you out rather than the other way around.

When my advisers came back from the challenge, they were so proud of themselves because they had broken through that four letter word that had been holding them back for so long. Once that happened and once they realised that people out there really did want their services, they were converting clients left, right and centre. As I speak, I continuously get emails from my business advisers saying how they have converted yet another client for their personal consulting business.

I share this story with you in the hopes that it will help you recognise that there are some thought processes and self-limiting beliefs that are holding you back from what you want to achieve. Now, it could be your loved one telling you that you're crazy and asking why you're spending all the money or why you are taking so many risks in the business or it could be the same challenge I had when I was worried about putting on extra staff because that meant I would need to have extra work to keep them busy. That's a big responsibility. Whatever it is, if you can take 100% responsibility and be honest with yourself and recognise that fear, you have taken the biggest leap possible in your journey towards becoming a multi-millionaire.

Recognising that fear is the first step but confronting the fear, embracing the fear and overcoming the fear is the transformational moment that I want you to strive for. Here's something to cheer you up. I promise you, everyone on the planet experiences fear. Yes, even me. I can assure you that before Donald Trump makes a major investment, he has collywobbles in his stomach. Before Richard Branson decides to take on a major project, he has collywobbles in his stomach. Before James Packer decided to build major casinos and divest himself of his media interest, he had major collywobbles in his stomach. Every successful person on the planet experiences fear. The only individuals that don't experience fear are those individuals that aren't pushing themselves.

Let's face it. You see top sportsmen out there performing superhuman feats and doing quadruple somersaults in the air or snowboarding down a mountain at a million miles an hour but if you don't think that they experience fear every time they try a new technique or master a new strategy, you're dreaming. We all go through it. The difference is that the one who has the courage to confront their fear and push through the barrier is the one who's going to succeed. This again is why 92.5% of business owners do not do more than a million dollars in turnover, because they're not willing to face their fear. They're not willing to take the next step. They're not willing to get serious about building a multi-million dollar organisation and having the things they truly want in life.

INCONVENIENT TRUTH

Here are some inconvenient truths for you to ask yourself:

What fear is holding you back from achieving what you want in life?

What action steps are you going to take to overcome that fear?

What assistance are you going to seek to ensure that you break through that fear and transform yourself into the person you know you can become?

CHAPTER 8

Creating Customers For Life

CHAPTER 8

Creating Customers For Life

The Multi-Million Dollar Secret

At the time of writing this book, I have built five multi-million dollar companies, generated well over $60 million but probably closer to $70 million in my companies and am able to generate as many clients as I desire for my organisations. Why is it that I can break through the statistics and have these results when 92.5% of my competitors can't?

Well, I just revealed one of the biggest stumbling blocks for business owners and that is their own personal fear which prevents them from taking the challenge to become as successful as they deserve to be. The other reason for my success is that I have developed the skills to generate clients at will and most of my competitors haven't. This obviously gives me a huge advantage.

Now to be honest, I can't take all the credit for this skill and I want to explain how I managed to develop this ability. It is one of the most powerful skills you can have because let's face it, if you have the ability to create as many clients as you want, when you want, there is no limit to the success that you can achieve.

How did I develop this skill? Well, for the mechanical processes you use in sales, I studied with the best in the world. People like Brian Tracy, Tim Hopkins and Chet Holmes to name a few. But for my real ability to sell, I have to confess quite honestly that it was my mother who developed my natural skill. Please let me explain by briefly sharing my mother's story with you. Trust me, there is a very powerful life lesson in this chapter, so please read this carefully.

You see, my mother lived in the middle of nowhere, near a town called Mumble. In fact, she was about 30 miles away from the town of Mumble living in a forest with her family, trying to eke out a living on the land. More than that, when you think of a home where someone lives, you think of four walls and a roof and maybe a toilet. Well, my mother had none of those. My mother's house was a bag hut made of hessian bags. Yes, the sort of material that you carry grain in. It had sisalation on the roof, which was poisonous, so you couldn't collect the rainwater off the roof. Mum had to walk 100 metres to a little creek to get water for the house. She lived in this small bag hut with her mother, her father and her 2 sisters.

Now, that's pretty tough going and it wasn't that long ago, only 80 years that we're talking about. More than that, you can appreciate that my mother wouldn't have had a lot given to her in life. I mean, she hardly ever saw a book. The only way her father talked to her was through a leather strap across her legs. The reality was that there were not many material things in my mother's family.

At the grand age of 12 years old, my mother was kicked out of that bag hut and sent to work scrubbing floors for a doctor in Dubbo. Imagine this 12 year old girl hopping onto a train and going to a town that is bigger than anything she has ever seen and working for a stranger that she has never met. You would think that when she worked scrubbing floors as a cleaner for a doctor maybe her life would get a bit better materialistically but her bed was actually a cot outside on the veranda of the house where the doctor worked.

Life gets more challenging for her because at the age of 14, while she was washing some clothes for the doctor, her hand got stuck in one of those old fashioned washing machines with the rollers that squeezed the water out of the wet clothes and she lost her left hand. It was amputated at the wrist so it got bandaged up and she was packed off back to her mother and father that night as damaged goods.

That night, while she still had blood coming out of the stump of the left hand that she no longer had, her father started yelling at her because she did not get up from the dinner table and help her mother with the dishes. He barked at her and asked her what sort of girl she was to let her mother do the dishes on her own.

Now, in retrospect, perhaps her father may have been trying to help my mum learn a life lesson saying, "Get over yourself. So you've lost your hand. You've still got another one. You're not useless. Get out there and use what assets you still have." Perhaps that was the reason behind my grandfather yelling at my mother that night. I will never know. The reason I tell you this story is because my mother raised me on her own after she divorced my father and because my mother didn't have much in life, she learned to appreciate the things that she did have. She also learned to look out for others and help others because she knew how tough life could be.

So while I was growing up, it was drummed into me that I should think about other people before myself and if I was ever caught being selfish or not thinking of others, not opening doors for people or not offering a seat to someone, not eating all my dinner and not sharing what I had with other people, my mother would get out the dreaded bamboo stick and she would get me to hold out my hand (which I didn't mind too much as they were pretty tough) while she hit it or hit me behind my legs (now I've got to tell you, that one hurt) because she was worried that I would turn into a very selfish and unappreciative child.

When you think about the upbringing that my mother had, you can understand why she raised me the way she did. I love my mum, she's the most wonderful woman in the whole world and I can't thank her enough for the way that she raised me.

Unknown to her, because she instilled in me the importance of thinking of others rather than myself, it gave me this ability to automatically think of how I can help somebody else solve their problems. Whenever I see someone, my instincts always make me wonder how I can help that person. What can I do to assist that individual? Is there anything I can do to make their life better? It is an automatic reflex.

How does that help me be a super salesperson? How does that help me create more clients than my competition can? Well, it's quite simply because I don't try to sell anything to anyone. When somebody has a problem, it is my instinct to want to help them solve that problem. Now, it just so happens that when I solve that problem, I do it at a profit. When was the last time you wanted to be sold something? Well, the answer is probably never. Nobody likes to be sold anything but how do you like it when somebody offers to help you? Is that a nice sensation? Isn't it a good feeling when you know that you've got someone who's got your interests at heart and wants to assist you to achieve what you want to achieve?

Now, wait for it guys, here is the massive lesson.

You shouldn't be trying to sell what that you have.

What you should be doing is trying to determine the problems that your prospects are facing in life. Try to determine the best solutions for those prospects and then provide the very best solution you can to resolve that issue for them.

Now, if you take this philosophy to heart and you stop selling your products and you start thinking about what the problems are that your clients are facing, a whole new perspective will open up to you as to how you should be approaching, talking and communicating with your customers. You'll notice that you start to get a different reaction from the prospects that you're talking to because they'll realise that you are not there just to flog your wares to them and to separate them from their wallet but that you are there with a genuine interest to give them the very best solution to the problem that they have at the time.

Now this my friends, is a multi-million dollar secret. If you embrace this inconvenient truth along with the others that I've shared with you throughout this book, you will start to attract more money, more wealth and more success into your life than you ever dreamed possible.

KEEP YOUR CUSTOMERS FOR LIFE

As strange as it may sound, even though I've just told you the huge advantage that I have over my competition when it comes to acquiring clients, I don't want your major focus in your business to be on continuously generating new clients because the fact is that it costs you seven times more to get a new client than it does to sell to an existing one. Knowing this fact, it makes a lot more sense for you to maximise the value that you gain from your existing clients and look after them as well as you possibly can rather than continually go out and find new clients.

I find over and over again in businesses that I start working with, that the money and the effort is focused on getting new clients but very little attention is given to the people that they have already sold to. Please understand what you have accomplished when you have made the first sale. The client has said, "Hey, I trust you. Please, look after me and don't let me down."

You may think that when you make a sale to a new client, that's when your job ends but that's actually when your job starts. When you have a new person that has trusted you and handed over their money to you and said, "Okay, I'll give you the chance to show me what you've got," that is your huge chance to grab that client, nurture that client, get to know that client and help them with every problem and challenge known to man.

When they've handed over their money, you have accomplished one of the biggest and toughest challenges on the planet and that is, you have generated trust with them. They have trusted you to solve their problem for them and now is your chance to prove that that trust was not misplaced. Before you start looking at your marketing strategy and saying, "How can I get a hundred more clients to come into my business?" why don't you use a portion of those same resources that you were going to spend on buying new clients, to invest in your existing clients and show them how much you appreciate them and give them gifts and show them the love that they deserve for being part of your world?

IT IS OK TO HAVE A BIG BACKEND

In my air conditioning company, when most of my competitors were continually trying to just get new clients, I understood this principle of keeping a customer for life. When my competitors did an air conditioning installation, generally ducted air conditioning because that was my specialty, nine times out of ten they wouldn't even communicate with the client after the installation or offer them an annual service at the end of each year, which air conditioning systems honestly need.

On top of that, they wouldn't contact the clients in the future to see if there was anything else that they could help them with. The end result was that my competitors would possibly get $1,500 to $2,000 profit from a ducted air conditioning installation.

I, on the other hand, being streetsmart, would go in there with the strategic goal of not only wanting to sell them air conditioning but also a lot of other services in the future because once I had put in a great air conditioning system and shown them that I keep my word, it gave me the right to then offer them other products. Let me explain how this works. When I had my air conditioning company, the average rate that companies would charge to do an annual service on an air conditioning system was $120.

I decided, in my wisdom, that I could offer them an extraordinary annual service and for that people would be willing to pay $365.00. This is basically triple the going rate but for that to happen it had to be an extraordinary annual service, not just a run of the mill experience. Rather than just offer them an annual service, I offered them a ten year parts and labour warranty on their system. I offered to be there within two hours if they called. If we were not there within two hours I would pay them $200. If I couldn't fix the air conditioning system when I arrived, I would provide another air conditioning system for them so that they would never be hot or cold in their home again and it didn't matter if it was 12pm on Christmas Day with 50 degree heat, if their air conditioning broke down, we would be there to fix it.

Because I was offering such an incredible service to them and a ten year parts and labour warranty, rather than charge $120 a year, I charged them $1 a day, which was $365 a year. For that $365, they were treated like absolute royalty, as all your clients should be, and I got to deduct that fee from their credit card on a monthly basis. Instead of having the phone ring off the hook just before summer started with everybody under the sun wanting their air conditioning serviced, I had a cash flow stream and I had a system where I got to choose when to do the annual services instead of letting the clients choose when and I created, just in that division, a huge money-making business and an ongoing cash flow.

On top of that, the news gets better. Not only did I get my $2,000 profit for the installation of the air conditioning but over the next ten years I would get $3,650 from the annual servicing for the clients. I would also send out a newsletter to my clients. That newsletter would not be me flaunting my wares, it would be me sharing helpful information about how they could be doing things to keep improving their home.

Because I built the trust with my clients in the beginning, that gave me the opportunity to then offer them different products and services like individual temperature control in different rooms. It gave me the chance to offer them infrared switches that could be put in their houses to save electricity. It gave me the opportunity, when there was the big water scare with Waragamba Dam in Sydney, to offer imported reverse osmosis water filters to my clients because I wanted to make sure that they didn't get contaminated water. It gave me the chance to offer them air purifiers to prevent hayfever and the list goes on.

You can see that my competitors were getting $2,000 profit for a client but in many cases, the lifetime value of a client to me was $6,000 in profit. When you look at it, don't you think that it's far better for you to get three times the amount of money from a client as well as help them because if you're looking after them, you will do the best job for them? As we all know, there are good companies and bad companies out there.

There are sharks and disreputable individuals that will rip clients off and be proud of it. I know you who are reading this book are not one of them however, it is your responsibility to protect your client and to ensure they're not getting taken advantage of and to give them the very best service and solutions possible within your power.

When you understand this principle, rather than you continually going out to find new clients, you will focus on developing a backend and then you'll find that you have hundreds of thousands of dollars in hidden profits sitting in your company, just waiting to be picked up and you will have a hard time wiping the smile off your face.

INCONVENIENT TRUTH

Are you constantly searching for new clients?

When was the last time you thanked your existing clients?

Have you developed a backend for your company?

Are you maximising the lifetime value of your clients?

CHAPTER 9

The 7 Inconvenient Truths Why Most Business Owners Do Not Become Multi-Millionaires

CHAPTER 9

The 7 Inconvenient Truths Why Most Business Owners Do Not Become Multi-Millionaires

I hope you have enjoyed, no, actually I hope you have learned these principles that I have shared and are starting to apply them in what you are currently doing in your business. I would now like to share the 7 reasons why most people don't become multi-millionaires in business. Here are the inconvenient truths and even though they may make you feel uncomfortable, if you are honest with yourself and you acknowledge these principles and you apply them, the results in your business are more than likely going to double, triple, quadruple and whatever the heck comes after that.

How do I know? Well, not only do I apply this in every business that I have built and remember, each one has become a multi-million dollar organisation but I have helped many other people become millionaires and multi-millionaires in business by applying these same principles to their companies. So, if you need help, I'm more than happy to see if we can guide you in implementing these same inconvenient truths in your organisation.

INCONVENIENT TRUTH **Number 1**

The first inconvenient truth is that you can have the life you want but you must have the courage to get it.

Do not spend your life dreaming and wishing, saying, "I'm going to do this," or, "I'll get around to it." There is no time like the present. If you want to change your life, the ideal time to do it is now. Not tomorrow, not next week, not next year. Let's face it. Most people out there who are broke, are broke because they want to be broke. I know that I will get abused for that statement but they mostly have the same opportunities as you and I and rather than make the decision to study some course or book for an hour, they would rather watch X Factor on their massive, big screen TV that they have bought from Harvey Norman with 60 months interest free. That's their choice. Your choice, hopefully, is that you decided to study and add focus on a core skill that will help you gain more market share and reach the goals you set for yourself. Your choice!

Most people who are fat want to be fat. Why is that? Well, the last time I looked, nobody I've seen has walked along and accidentally tripped over and landed on a piece of chocolate cake that's fallen into their mouth. The reality is, if you want to be fitter and healthier, eat less, drink more and do some exercise. It's as simple as that. However, people don't like facing the inconvenient truth and so they will make excuses as to why they are where they are and as a result, they end up where they are. If you want to be broke, be honest and decide to be broke but if you want to be wealthy, be honest and decide to be wealthy. Both choices are correct and I'm not judging which one is right and which one is wrong but I know which one works better for me and I hope that you will make the right choice for you.

INCONVENIENT TRUTH **Number 2**

Before you can have the things that you want in life, you must have absolute clarity and belief that you know that what you are creating is what you really want. I mean absolute clarity, so if you say that you want a big house or you want a nice house, don't just call it a "nice house," go and search for the perfect house that you want. Get absolute clarity on what it looks like. Know exactly how much it costs. Know what suburb it is in. How many bedrooms does it have? Do you want a swimming pool? Do you want acreage?

Get clarity on the things that you want and then believe that you are worthy to have them. Have the absolute unshakable faith that you deserve these things in life and that you will do whatever it takes to get them. Once you develop that clarity and you have the belief that you are worthy of these things that you are chasing, you must then develop a clear plan or to put it another way, develop your goals, so that you can implement action steps to achieve the dreams that you want. Do not let anybody tell you that you can't do something. That's for you to decide. Nobody else. Never ever tell yourself no. Let somebody else do that for you.

INCONVENIENT TRUTH **Number 3**

You must develop success habits. Success is a habit just like value is a habit and it all starts the minute dawn breaks. Do you get up bright and early and plan your day and have clear thoughts about the actions that you're going to take to achieve your goals or do you make every excuse to stay under the covers and hit the snooze button and leave it till the last minute before you jump out of bed which you only do because you have to pay the bills? These are habits and it is easy to replace bad habits with good habits if you are serious and if you want something bad enough.

Now, to help you develop these success habits, I strongly urge you to find a proven mentor in your niche. Now, in business, you should find somebody who's at least five times more successful than you are, so that you can have them guide you and hold you accountable to do the things that you must do in your company and to be focusing on the right things that you're working on, not the 80% of things that don't provide you with results and rewards in your business.

One of the biggest benefits that I have had in my journey is being able to find the right mentors to fast-track my success although it did not seem like it at the time. I had massive arguments with the most important person in the world to me, which is my wife, because at the time, she did not understand how critical my self-education was to our future success. Please, develop your success habits, find a mentor and invest in yourself.

INCONVENIENT TRUTH **Number 4**

You must have the right business vehicle. Remember the magic formula that I shared with you earlier? For a great business, you should have fantastic maths, plus great psychology, plus a sunrise business, minus a sunset business, plus lifestyle. You must look at these five features, these five characteristics in an organisation to determine whether you're in a racing car that will get you to your destination quickly or if you're in a jalopy.

Now, use the analogy of a taxi driver and how he has kept his income. Even though he's working very hard for 12 hours a day, 6 and 7 days a week, he has a capped income to what he is doing. It's probably not the best industry to get into. He is also in a sunset business because technology will probably make drivers obsolete within the next 5 to 10 years. Sometimes it's not easy to look at your own business and admit that your baby is ugly but if you don't have great maths and you don't have great psychology and you have got a poor lifestyle and you are in a sunset business, you don't have to be Einstein to work out that maybe you should be getting into a different business vehicle.

Please be honest with yourself because let's face it, if you've been in business for 3 to 5 years and you're not at least a millionaire yet, then you're obviously doing something wrong and time is ticking away. There are thousands of opportunities in the world. Don't get emotionally attached to your existing one. If it's an ugly baby, put it out of its misery and move on to a better vehicle.

INCONVENIENT TRUTH **Number 5**

Create a customer for life. This is one of the biggest advantages I have always had over my competitors. See, this is the only time I give you permission to have a big backend. What do I mean by that? Well, in your business, once you have done your initial transaction with a customer, remember that it's not where your job ends. That's where your job starts. What you want to do when you get a client is get to find out as much as you can about your client. Go deep. Work out all of the problems that they are facing. Develop the right solution for them and help them solve it, for life.

If you go through this process and you focus on developing trust, having a relationship and offering solutions to their needs, you will more than likely triple, quadruple and quintuple etc. your business. The other big benefit of this is that you will start to develop a natural word of mouth lead generation in your company because your friends will have no option but to tell other friends how wonderful you are. On a side note, I have not had the time in this book to explain the power of a million-dollar referral program. However, you must develop an effective, reliable referral program for your business.

INCONVENIENT TRUTH **Number 6**

You must develop the very best team around you. Many business owners are worried about hiring people that are smarter than they are or have more qualifications than they do. Perhaps they're upset because these individuals might make more money than they do. Well, all of this doesn't matter because the reality is that for you to get the job done, you need the very best people on your team to do it. Football teams that have the very best team win the grand final. The second best team is the runner up and the third best team, well, nobody even knows who they are. It's the same in business. The very best companies have the very best teams, the second best companies have the second best teams and the third best companies, well, they just simply go out of business.

Why don't people have the very best teams? Quite honestly, it's because of personalities and because many business owners aren't willing to hold their staff accountable. They are not willing to create standards that the staff must meet and they're not willing to monitor the efforts the staff put in to achieve the standard that the business owner desires. Many times, it's because of the negative self-talk that is going on with that little voice inside their head saying, "Oh, if you sack this person, you'll never find another one. This person knows so much that's critical to the success of the business. If I sack him, look at all the extra work I will have to do."

I am telling you, from someone that's had a $10,000,000 education, that if you do not remove the worst people from your company and if you do not hold your staff accountable and create standards that they must meet, then you will pay the ultimate price. You are the leader of your organisation. Your job is to find the very best team, to give them the very best resources, to give them the very best training and to monitor the results that your very best team are achieving for you.

INCONVENIENT TRUTH **Number 7**

The final inconvenient truth, which is by far and away the most important, is fear. This is such a devastating word. It does deserve to be a four letter word. If I was allowed to add a few other four letter words in here to emphasise my abhorrence of this emotion, well then, I would add them because fear is responsible for so many people with so much potential never pushing through those barriers that we all have, to get to the other side. Quite honestly, I feel they are ripping off society because they are not reaching their potential. They are not just hurting their lifestyle, they are not just hurting the families that they're not providing adequately for, they're ripping off society because who knows what things they can accomplish if they could eliminate fear and just say, "Screw it. Let's do it."

The ultimate example of this is Richard Branson, having the courage to create a galactic enterprise to send people up into space so that one day all of us will start to think of space travel as normal, just like we think of hopping on an aeroplane now. Imagine going from London to Sydney in one hour. Richard Branson never let fear dictate to him, and I bet you his underpants rose dramatically in his shorts when he decided to start Virgin Galactic, and the benefits to the world are simply immeasurable because this maverick entrepreneur confronted his fear and did the impossible and as I'm writing this book, he has nearly accomplished his goal of creating galactic travel for the average man and woman.

CHAPTER 10

The One Thing You Must Do To Transform Your Financial Future

CHAPTER 10

The One Thing You Must Do To Transform Your Financial Future

I've shared a lot of information in this book about the life lessons that have helped me achieve my successes and the reason why I named this book *"The Inconvenient Truth About Business Success: Why Most People Won't Become Multi-Millionaires And The One Thing You Can Do To Change That"* is because when you get serious about your success you have to face some inconvenient truths.

I have one more inconvenient truth for you and when you understand it, when you internalise it and when you believe it with all of your heart, this one truth will transform your life in ways that you can't even fathom right now. Nothing will be able to stop you because the results I see occurring with my students who apply this one thing, are truly spectacular.

Before I talk about this one life principle I want you to realise something and it is that it doesn't matter where you're born, it doesn't matter what sort of income you're on and it doesn't matter what age you are. There's something that happens to all of us from time to time and this very technical term is, "Shit happens."

You know that experience when you think your world's collapsing on you? You've got this sense of being overwhelmed and you're lying in bed at night in a cold sweat, wondering how you're going to be able to get through the next few hours, petrified of what's facing you. This traumatic experience happens to most people. In fact, when you're an entrepreneur, you'll probably experience this in your organisation every 3 to 4 months. Something major will occur that will make you feel like you just want a bus to run over you or you want to curl up in the foetal position and not get out of bed.

The reason this happens, I believe, is because the world is trying to teach you something. These are lessons that all of us must break through to grow.

For some reason known only to God, who I am sure has a warped sense of humour, it is time to learn something new and it is at these times that you determine the future of your life.

You have choices when these times get tough. You can give up (which is what most people do) or you can power through and receive the rewards for having the courage to do so.

The lesson that the world is trying to teach you is that you've been at this level for too long and you need another challenge.

The world says, "You've got to change what you're doing because your life is not as it's meant to be so I've put this obstacle in front of you to get you to climb to the next level in life."

I do not care if you are Richard Branson or Tony Robbins, breaking through the barriers and going into the unknown is downright scary for everyone. For most of us, when these crises and obstacles crop up, we wish we were someone else but the overriding principle to keep in mind when they occur is the one thing I'm about to reveal to you now.

TAKE 100% RESPONSIBILITY FOR YOUR SITUATION AND FACE IT HEAD ON!

The developed world has a plan for you and throughout your life you are being moulded and subtly expected to follow their plan for you so that you slot into the system.

You see, as you're growing up, right from when you popped out of your mother's womb, you had people looking after you. Mum was there to nurse you when you were sick. Your parents provided the dollars to buy the things that you needed. They told you what to eat. They told you what to wear, what to say and how to act. They taught you their world and their reality and how you are expected to perform in public.

Then you get into the school system where they categorise you and tell you what they think you should do with your life.

As you get older, because you've been cared for all of your life, by your parents, other family and your teachers, and your partner in many cases, you subconsciously come to the conclusion that someone else will take care of you.

In fact, 60% of the population is now receiving social welfare of some sort from the Australian government. We are trained on a very deep level to think that whatever happens in life, it'll be taken care of by somebody else. It's somebody else's responsibility. As you grow up, you get to a certain age and, depending on how your parents have raised you, you are given a story of how your life should pan out.

You are given a map or an outline of how your parents feel your life should turn out and a lot of you will go down that path and live out that life and stay in that reality but there are some of you, chances are that you are reading this book, that say, "Hell, no. I don't want this life. I don't want this reality. I deserve something better. I want something better." When you come to that decision, what is occurring is the principle of responsibility and this is the one thing, above all else, that will help you achieve whatever financial or life goal it is that you want to achieve. You see, 80% of the population are unwilling to take responsibility for their life, their actions and their decisions and as a result, the world will keep putting barriers and lessons in front of them and most times, they simply won't learn those lessons. Let me give you an example. The woman called Mrs. Liebeck.

This was a lady who accidentally spilled hot coffee on her lap while she was sitting in a car in the parking lot of a McDonalds store in America.

This woman decided that it was McDonald's fault that she tipped the lid off her coffee and spilled it all over her lap and burned herself. So, rather than learning the lesson that it is not a smart thing to do, she decided to blame someone else for her dilemma and sued McDonalds for $2.86 million. Here is another example of what I am talking about. One person in America, a 32 year old homeless man, sued his parents because he wanted to buy 2 Domino's pizza stores and expected his parents to sell their house to provide for him because he felt that his parents neglected him as a child and they would be proud of him if they saw him become successful in life.

This is what I'm referring to when I talk about responsibility. Time and time again, I see individuals who want to blame somebody or something else for what has occurred to them in their life but here's the inconvenient truth, if you don't like something, it's up to you to change it. You won't be able to change anything until you take 100% responsibility for the situation that has arisen.

The best example that I can give you is this: When I lost everything that I possessed and had my staff steal materials, time and labour from me (and we are talking millions of dollars) which resulted in me becoming bankrupt, for a time

I thought, "Woe is me. Life's unfair. How dare they steal from me? I will never go into business with staff again. Staff are evil." I held that thought for probably 3 to 4 months after the event until all of sudden, it dawned on me that it was my fault that they stole from me. I gave them the opportunity to steal from me. I didn't put systems in place in my organisation to hold the people accountable. I decided to turn a blind eye to what was going on because I didn't want to face those staff members and confront what my sixth sense was telling me was happening in my organisation.

Then I finally faced the reality that I was responsible. Yes, it was me that caused my bankruptcy. I was the reason I lost everything I worked my whole life for. When I took the responsibility for it, it actually lifted a massive weight off my shoulders because it also help me realise that although I'd just lost everything that I'd spent a lifetime creating, I still had the knowledge between my ears and the ability to create another organisation. I still had assets and skills that very few people have ever developed. So, why should I feel sorry for myself when I've learned all of these lessons in life? I should take advantage of the lessons and build another company. That is when I realised the power of taking responsibility and I went on to build another 4 multi-million dollar companies. Can you see that I had two choices? I could have carried on and blamed the world and talked about how unfair life is saying, "Nobody can get ahead in this world. It's all just rigged against us," or I could take the other path and say, "Well, that wasn't that much fun but what did I learn from this? How did I cause this to happen? I won't let it happen again."

What's occurring here is that you can either take responsibility for what's happening in your life or you can blame someone else but if you blame someone else for why you're not achieving the things that you want in life, you're not going to get where you want to go. You must accept that whatever situation you are in is because of the choices and the decisions that you have made. You take 100% responsibility for them and at that moment, when you take that responsibility and you accept that you are where you are because of the choices and decisions that you make, you realise that you are the master of your own destiny. No one else can control your life and you can have, do and get whatever it is that you set your mind to.

If you are serious about transforming your life then follow these 4 universal principles. You will find that all truly successful people follow these principles because they are success habits.

Whether it is Tony Robbins, Brian Tracy, Richard Branson, Donald Trump or Mark Bouris, we all follow these steps religiously in our lives and as a result, we get more out of life than many others.

1. **First, you see life as it really is**

Now, you've got to be honest with yourself.

If you're a chubby bubby and you've got those excess kilos around you, you can say to yourself, "Oh, well, it's because I'm big boned and my genetics forced me to be this way and I've got a slow metabolism." If that makes you feel better, well, go for it but you can say, "Well, I don't exercise and I eat the wrong food and I love my chocolate cake too much but I don't want to be fat any more so what I will do is I'll exercise more, I'll eat less and I'll drink more water." What has just occurred is that you've taken responsibility. You took responsibility for what you were doing that was making you fat and unhealthy and you made that decision to say, "I don't want to be fat and unhealthy any more. I want to be a lean, mean, love machine." You decide. You take responsibility and you start transforming yourself.

It is exactly the same with your financial position.

You can look at your bank account and you can say, "Well, I don't have much. I don't make enough money. I guess I'll always be broke" or you can take responsibility for the situation and you can say, "You know what? Out of every dollar I earn, I'm going to put 20% away into a savings account. I won't buy any more big screen TV's and I won't waste my money on eating out 4 times a week. I don't really need to take that cruise for $15,000.00, I would have as good a time getting away with the family here in Australia for only $2,000.00.

I'll be very frugal with my money and I'll put it into an investment account to get a reasonable rate of return and when I am 65 I will have $2,000,000 in the bank and have the best golden years ever.

You need to face the truth. If you don't want to be broke in retirement when you can't generate income, then do something now or decide to be broke! It's your choice, just don't complain about it.

2. **Be truthful about your situation**

For example, when you see life as it is.

Let me give you an example:

Let's just say that you own a video store and that for many years you've been making great money selling VHS videos and DVDs to people and then, bit by bit, your profits are starting to disappear.

You could say to yourself, "Oh, it's the market and things will get better. I've made money for the last 15 years selling these things. I'm sure it'll come good again" but every month you dip into the equity on your house to prop up the business until, over time, you finally have no equity, no house and probably no partner. (I usually find the trifecta is when the business finally fails).

Or, you could take responsibility and say, "Hey, this isn't good. This industry is not going to get any better. DVDs aren't going to make a comeback because people can watch any movie they want online now. I have to leave this business and either sell it or shut it down."

It may be unfair and it might be hard to deal with but you must get to the truth of the matter and you must take responsibility for it.

3. **Create a clear vision of your future**

This was explained in detail in chapter 3 of this book but the secret is that you must BELIEVE in your vision. It is no use just dreaming of something, you must be serious and DECIDE to HAVE this thing. Make it a burning commitment.

If that is you being a multi-millionaire, then get that vision of being a multi-millionaire. **Believe** that you can be a multi-millionaire.

Start working out a plan to become a multi-millionaire and when you do, it is time for the fourth step.

4. **Always have a mentor**

   The fourth step, and the most important one here, is to find a mentor that is a multi-millionaire in business. Look for someone you feel can guide you and assist you in achieving what you want to achieve. When you take responsibility for where you are in life and when you create a new vision for yourself and you believe in that vision, map out a plan and find a mentor that can help you execute that plan wisely, you will find that you will start to achieve your goals faster and more easily than you ever thought possible.

What I have shared with you is my personal journey that has taken me from frustration to freedom.

I hope you take these lessons and use them to achieve your goals and I do want to hear about your success stories. Hopefully we'll meet one day in my Streetsmart Business environment. Until then, I wish you all the best.

Yours sincerely,

Ian Marsh.

Please share what you think about this information on our Facebook page

Facebook.com/streetsmartmarketing1

ABOUT THE AUTHOR

Ian Marsh

Ian Marsh started showing business owners how to create their own million dollar businesses in 2006, after three desperate requests from a business owner on the Gold Coast called Jeremy Young. Jeremy was about to lose the trifecta of his business, his house and his marriage. After helping Jeremy implement some core strategies in his business and seeing the effect he had on this person's life, Ian then committed himself to showing other business owners how to create successful businesses as well.

He is someone who works with businesses every single day and finds hidden, overlooked profits they didn't even know they had. He is not a Harvard trained, MBA holding academic. He has gone through the school of hard knocks and experienced nearly every high and low you could possibly have in business, resulting in him becoming the Streetsmart Business owner.

Starting as an electrician and refrigeration mechanic he became a student of streetsmart marketing principles.

- ✓ From June 1999 until 2004 he built and grew Marsh Air conditioning P/L into a $12,000,000 a year business.
- ✓ WHOOPS! In December 2005 he had the rug pulled out from under him and went bankrupt due to a massive theft of time and material in the company.
- ✓ In January 2006 he built a new company. In 8 months he'd built it to see a turnover of $8,000,000pa. Not only that, he implemented a simple, yet little-known-system that slashed staff's sickies (just 5 out of 30 staff). Theft by staff zeroed down to nothing. (Marsh Marketing P/L).
- ✓ In March 2006 he launched a website www.aircondirect.com.au. This is Australia's most powerful air conditioning website. One of the first drop shipping websites created. (Not bad for a bloke who left home at 14).
- ✓ November 2006 saw him selling the above company for a BIG profit with four companies itching to purchase it ... the bidding wars began, upping the price as they fought to buy the business.
- ✓ In March 2006 he decided to show other tradesmen and small business owners his powerful strategies to build their businesses into million dollar companies.

- ✓ December 2007 he won "Rebellious Marketer on the Year" Awarded at Magnetic Marketing Ceremonies in Perth.

- ✓ In March 2009 he moved to Perth to help Mal Emery build The Streetsmart Marketing Organisation to help entrepreneurs create the lifestyle and business they want to achieve.

- ✓ In August 2010 he launched Streetsmart Business School for Serious Entrepreneurs.

- ✓ In January 2011 he created the Streetsmart Business Adviser Program which has helped many individuals create 6 and 7 figure incomes and has helped numerous individuals create successful consulting businesses by learning his consulting strategies.

- ✓ **October 2013 to the present, Ian owns Streetsmart Marketing International, one of the most results oriented Business Coaching programs in existence today.**

WORKBOOK

On the 29th of May 1953, two mountaineers, Sir Edmund Hillary and Tenzing Norgay did what hundreds before them had failed to do. They successfully summited Mount Everest unassisted by oxygen. Hillary and Norgay did not accidentally stumble upon the peak of Everest, their planning started years earlier. Their goal crystal clear. From the moment the idea had formed in their minds, a precise plan was developed – followed by thousands of small steps, each one taking them closer to that moment of achievement.

What do you really want in life?

> The starting point of all achievement is desire. Keep this constantly in mind. Weak desires bring weak results, just as a small amount of fire makes a small amount of heat.

Napoleon Hill

It's time to get clarity, 'connect the dots' and put in place the steps you need to take towards achieving your ultimate business and lifestyle goals.

This workbook has been designed to be worked through in conjunction with your ***'StreetSmart Business Success Club' EPISODE ONE*** DVD

Missing your DVD? Phone 1300 881 671 for immediate support.

To achieve business success, you must first have absolute clarity on what 'success' looks like to you. Thomas J. Stanley and William D. Danko, authors of "The Millionaire Next Door" who studied 7.8 million millionaires to get their findings were asked in an interview how most people became millionaires. Their answer was quite surprising.

"Most millionaires own their own business and invest in other businesses and they are willing to work harder than their competitor."

I urge you to complete this module at a time when you can allocate 100% uninterrupted concentration. Ideally, leave the office and take a few days to yourself. Book a room in a hotel or find a space where you can immerse yourself and find clarity as you search inwards. Go to your happy place. This time is critical to helping you shape your dream future.

It is time to get serious about your business.

Exercise One: Define Your Dreams

To find success you must first have absolute clarity about what ultimate 'success' would look and feel like to you - because everyone's dreams are uniquely their own.

Write in detail, how your perfect day would look without limitations or consequences. Include small details so you feel like you're inside your 'perfect day.' This will become your 'core dream' and allow you to start making decisions that get you closer to living this day.

i.e. The alarm goes off at 6.15am, I smile at my wife lying next to me. Past her happy sleepy form I can see uninterrupted views of the ocean lapping at the shore with the sun just peeking through. I leap out of bed, refreshed and full of energy. My house sits on Beach Cove Lane. I'm a stone's throw from the beach and slip into my training gear for my morning run. I'm fit, healthy and love to start my day this way seeking clarity about what the day will bring. I run fast because I'm excited about new ideas and can't wait to get to the office to start exploring them. Etc....

Include as many details as possible, such as what your house looks like, what car you are driving, what you do for fun, what you have for breakfast, what your relationship looks like, what your perfect client looks like...etc.

Exercise Two: Break Down Your Goals

List your key goals from your story here.

Remember, ***you can have ANYTHING you want in this world.*** *Do not censor your dreams based on how it may affect others. This is about YOUR future.*

When listing your goals, drill down to the specifics.

For example, if your goal is to own a BMW 7 Series for $200,000. Go to the dealership, work out your monthly repayments. Choose the colour, the extras etc... make it real.

If you have included your dream home, then work out what the monthly mortgage repayments will be. You will need this specific information to complete the next section of your workbook.

Lifestyle Goals

______________________________Deadline______________

______________________________Deadline______________

______________________________Deadline______________

______________________________Deadline______________

______________________________Deadline______________

Family Goals

__________________________________Deadline________________

__________________________________Deadline________________

__________________________________Deadline________________

__________________________________Deadline________________

__________________________________Deadline________________

Business Goals

__________________________________Deadline________________

__________________________________Deadline________________

__________________________________Deadline________________

__________________________________Deadline________________

__________________________________Deadline________________

List your health goals here. I've have included a 'pros and cons' column so you can easily see the things you want to 'begin or keep' and the habits you would like to break. This way you can easily eliminate the negatives from your daily rituals.

Health Goals

Pros________________________ Cons______________________

Pros________________________ Cons______________________

Pros________________________ Cons______________________

Pros________________________ Cons______________________

Pros________________________ Cons______________________

Pros________________________ Cons______________________

Pros________________________ Cons______________________

Pros________________________ Cons______________________

Exercise Three: Refine Your Goals

It's time to put your blinkers on. Choose the one most important goal from each category.

LIFESTYLE

What one thing will have the most impact on your life when it comes to your lifestyle?

FAMILY

What one thing will have the most impact on your life when it comes to family?

BUSINESS

What one thing will have the most impact on your life when it comes to business?

HEALTH

What one thing will have the most impact on your life when it comes to health?

Write down your key goal from each category that will have the most impact, then concentrate only on those as your top priority.

LIFESTYLE ______________________________

____

____

FAMILY ______________________________

____

____

BUSINESS ______________________________

____

____

____

HEALTH ______________________________

____

____

Exercise Four: Reverse Engineer Your Goals

Now that you know what you want, it's time to work out how to achieve it. This is where you create your 'roadmap to success' by determining the steps you need to take.

This is where the rubber meets the road and you need to be very honest if your current business is going to be the right vehicle to get you to where you want to be. It's time to determine whether you're driving a jalopy or a racing car.

How's the math in your business?
Is there a good margin?
Is there good profit?
Is there a hungry crowd who want what you're selling?
Are you in a sunrise business or a sunset business?

Take your monetary goals above and put them through this simple formula to see if they are achievable or if you need to reassess your 'vehicle for success.'

EXAMPLE:

Say you have an income goal of $300,000 per year.
Your business sells widgets at $25,000 per unit with a $5,000 profit margin.
To reach your income goal, you would have to sell 60 units per year.
You know you need 3 leads to sell 1 unit.
So you would need 180 leads a year.
(48 weeks a year. Must generate 4 leads per week)

Is this realistic? YES!

Use the space opposite to reverse engineer your monetary goals using the same process.

If your business at peak is making you just $100,000 per year, then you need to change the way you're doing business to reach your goals. It's time to take action!

Exercise Five: Create Your Vision Board

Use these pages to paste images or words that help bring your vision to life...

Keep your vision board close and refer to it daily to ensure your key goals are at the forefront of your mind. If you have a clear picture of what you're aiming for, you will start to subconsciously make decisions that will guide you closer to that end goal.

IN SUMMARY

Taking the time create your dream lifestyle and business vision and take the steps towards living the life you truly aspire to. With time whizzing past at a rate of knots, don't wake up asking yourself 'where have the last 10 years gone?'

Now is the time to take action and TAKE CONTROL of your life.

- ☐ ***Have you*** *worked out a clear picture of what you want?*
- ☐ ***Do you*** *believe you can have it?*
- ☐ ***Have you*** *worked out what's enabling your life and what's inhibiting it?*
- ☐ ***Have you*** *determined the top 5 things you can have that will most impact your life?*
- ☐ ***Have you*** *determined whether your business is a jalopy or a racing car?*
- ☐ ***Have you*** *reverse engineered your goals and developed your action plan to achieve them?*

Need help turning your business into a racing car? The StreetSmart Marketing team is here to help. Call our team today on 1300 881 671 and find out how to ensure you are on the path to success.

RESOURCES

Business Success Tool

STREETSMART CENTURION COACHING

Imagine what you could accomplish working one-on-one with a business coach that has created 5 multi-million dollar businesses

The **StreetSmart Centurion Program** combines the full power of the StreetSmart Marketing team and faculty to create a complete 'Done For You' marketing system ready to deploy into your business.

Ian Marsh only works with 4 private clients at a time who are referred to as 'Centurions' and are part of Ian's inner sanctum. Every Centurion that has followed Ian's advice to the letter has achieved from 200% - 1500% improvements in their business.

Along with personal coaching, the Centurion program includes a selection of StreetSmart products including:

✓ The **Business Mastery Training Program**
✓ **StreetSmart Business School** attendance

If you are serious about taking your business to the next level then applying for the Centurion coaching program could be the next step in helping you achieve your ultimate goals of business and lifestyle success.

To find out if Centurion Coaching is right for you call **1300 881 671**